HOW TO TEACH CHILDREN
The Wonder of Sex

DR. AND MRS. J.C. WILLKE

HAYES PUBLISHING CO., INC.
6304 Hamilton Avenue
Cincinnati, Ohio 45224

1st Edition
Paperback

1st Edition, October, 1964
11th Printing, October, 1969

Pocketbook

1st Printing, January, 1971
5th Printing, October, 1979

Hardbound

1st Edition, October, 1966
3rd Printing, January, 1970

Second Edition
Paperback, January, 1983

Library of Congress Catalog Card No. 66-28985

ISBN 0-910728-00-3 (1st edition)
ISBN 0-910728-17-8 (revised edition)

Available From

HAYES PUBLISHING CO.

Cincinnati, Ohio 45224

Phone (513) 681-7559

Our thanks to
our parents

Contents

4. Attitudes   49

Our Mixed-up Heritage on Sex Attitudes • A Wife's Duty? • Sex Is Sacred • Who Married You? • Christians Believe • Proud of Sex • Pride of Manhood and Womanhood • Breasts • Nurse in Public! • Expose Yourself to Nurse? • In Front of My Son? • Why Nurse? • Advantages: *To Mother, To Baby, To Dad* • A Secure, Contented Child • Bodies Are Holy

5. Love   59

What Is Love? • Love Our Neighbor • Love God • Love My Husband or Wife • Strange World, Isn't It! • So, What Is Love — Really? • Love Is Giving • Not Selfish • But Everybody Says • Crumbs from the Table • Reverie • Wake Up! • Key • Teach Your Children? • In Front of Them? • Show Them: *Does She? Does He? Do They?* • Not All Sex? • In a Parked Car? • Protect Your Children

6. Teen-age Marriages   71

Early Marriage vs. Education • Teen-age Marriages — What Chance For Happiness? • Your Advice • Earlier Dating — More Illegitimacy • Why Is All This Happening?

7. Building Blocks   77

Why Teen-agers Have Sex • Effect of Social Customs • Toys Teach • Dress like Mom • Hair • Nylons and Little Heels • Training Bra! • Charm School • School or Church Dances • Girls Sooner Than Boys • Dating in Grade School • The Next Logical Step — Sex! • The Spark • We Started It! • Popular? • Like a Flower

8. What to Do   87

How to Stop the Push into Premature Adulthood • Give Them Constructive Activities • Athletics • Camping, Service, and Scouting Groups • When Should They Start? • Other Constructive Activities • Psychosexual Identity

9. When They Date   95

When Should They Date? • Going Steady • Movies • TV • Drinking • Driving • Dress of Teen-agers • Late Hours • Prom Night • Skating Parties, Football Games, Etc. • Slumber Parties • This Means You

The Willke Family, 1964
L. to r.: Anne, Chuck, Theresa, Marie, Joe, Dr. Willke, Mrs. Willke, Timmy.

The Willke Family, 1983
Standing: Bill and Theresa Wilka, Tim, Carol and Chuck Willke, Joe. Seated:
Bob and Marie Meyers with Stephan, Mrs. Willke, Dr. Willke, Anne.

Foreword

Hello — we are a happy husband and wife, parents of six, small to large, healthy children and call Cincinnati, Ohio, our home. We lead an interesting life which includes a busy medical practice, teaching and rearing our children, and being involved in many extra-curricular commitments in the fields of medicine, family life organization, speaking, etc.

We are as surprised as anybody that we wrote this book. We really didn't have time, but found ourselves simply taking the time because we felt strongly the need for these things to be written.

For a variety of reasons, in recent years, we have found ourselves more and more being asked to speak to groups of students, parents, teachers, and professional people on the subject of sex, its great dignity, and the proper education of children on this most important subject.

We soon found that, after discussing these things with a group, we would then want to recommend some reading to further their knowledge and encourage them to follow through. Over the last several years we have made, we think, a diligent search of the available literature to find the book, particularly for parents, that we needed. Our search and readings have certainly helped us and broadened our knowledge in the field, and we must pay our sincere thanks to these writers.

However, each current book was either too long or too short, too technical or too childish, too prudish or too irreverent, too clerical or too secular, too mechanical, too medical, too psychological, or too expensive. We feel that we are practical, everyday parents, who happen to be medically and psychologically knowledgeable, and who are conscious of God's real presence in our lives. We wanted something that was "just plain vanilla."

We are convinced sex education of children is the job of parents. Nothing is more evident to us than that to do this job right is far from easy. Furthermore, to apply these facts in a constructive, guiding way as the children approach and enter their teens is really difficult.

Our message, we hope, will know no religious or social boundary. We welcome our Jewish friends since we sincerely owe them an age-old debt of gratitude for the dignity of marriage and the other family ideals we have inherited from them and still share with them. To our highly respected Christian friends of many persuasions, both clerical and lay, we feel that, with almost no exceptions, you will find our thoughts to be your own. We have found almost no incompatibility with other Americans, regardless of faith, when we share these problems together. We sincerely welcome everyone to join us in considering them.

So we have the boldness to suggest that this is, at least partly, an answer to what we felt was a need.

Our major qualifications as experts?

We are parents.

We are concerned.

We are deeply in love.

                                        Jack and Barbara Willke

Preface to Second Edition

Nearly twenty years have passed since this book's publication. Since that time, much has happened in the world, in our nation, and in our family. Basically, people haven't changed. We're still boys and girls, men and women, single and married. We still, as individuals, have the same need to be loved, to feel secure, to be wanted, to feel pleasure and joy, to be happy.

Many speak of a sexual revolution over these past two decades and certainly there have been changes, some good, some bad. The increase in pre- and extramarital sex, of divorce, and of family fragmentation is obvious to everyone. Many are unaware or unconcerned that almost every nation in the Western world has seen its birth rate drop and remain below replacement level for over a decade now with the result that all of our populations are aging rapidly.

Abortion is legal, increasing steadily, and now claims the life of almost every third baby conceived in the USA.

Homosexuality in our lifetime has changed from a crime to be punished, to an illness to be treated, to a deviance to be tolerated, to a variant to be accepted, to an alternative form of life style, to a glorified choice of life style, to an aggressive and militant social and political movement.

The feminist movement, with all of its justified and long-overdue reach for equality, found itself led by radicals who clearly moved well beyond the goals of the great majority of American women, became almost counterproductive, and has begun to reassess its goals.

Sex education, formerly the exclusive province of home and church, was introduced into schools, was thrown out of many, and has since been slowly reinstated in most. It has remained intensely controversial in some areas. Becoming a major thrust of public clinics, the well-known "Planned Parenthood" program, in spite of heavily funded saturation efforts, has failed to stop the rise of illegitimate pregnancy, abortion, and V.D. This failure is so obvious that many are asking whether such a solution hasn't in actuality become part of the problem.

Is the family as we know it dying? We think not. The decay is obvious, but still sixty-seven per cent of minor children live with their two biological parents, thirteen per cent with one biological and one step parent, and an additional seventeen per cent with a single parent.*

We believe that the family is alive and well, showing its resiliency under these new challenges. In spite of the ongoing tragedy of all too frequent divorce, men and women continue to marry at the highest rate in our history. They continue to seek that love and solace, that companionship and security, that joy and fulfillment that can be found only in the loving embrace of a good marriage.

Will your children find it? Can you help them to find that hoped-for, one faithful partner with whom they will want to spend a lifetime? Can you help to shape them so that they will be able, through their learned (from you) ability, to give unselfishly of themselves to their partner, and also receive the love and support each will need so much? Will they choose

---

*Washington *Times*, October 13, 1982, AP Analysis.

wisely in the first place and then foster that love through the years so that it can, as it must, grow and mature?

Much depends upon you and how you witness in front of them, teaching them what marriage is and ought to be. You can help them. You can guide them. We hope that is what this book is all about.

So far, it has worked for us. With fingers crossed, we daily thank our Creator for the blessing our children have been to us. We are proud to see four happily married (we are grandparents) and two still in college. Our girls? A physician, an attorney, and a nurse. Our boys? An airplane pilot, a prospective professor, and a college freshman. Each is as different as night from day. Each has been a treasure beyond price. We are just as proud of our three sons-in-law and one daughter-in-law. Most of all, however, we have had each other for thirty-five enriching years.

So, almost twenty years later, having studied much, written much, traveled and lectured much, our chief qualifications remain that

we are parents,

we are concerned,

and we are ever more deeply in love.

Jack and Barbara Willke

1

Who Tells

It Was Good Enough for Us — Therefore —

First of all — is the kind of sex education that you, or your parents, or your grandparents received good enough for your children today? Let's not be deluded; let's be very straight about this fact. It might have been possible fifty years ago for a girl to marry without knowing the sexual facts of life and yet, perhaps, to make a reasonably happy adjustment. This is simply impossible today. Just think for a minute of customs before World War I. If an eighteen-year-old girl went on a date, she probably had a chaperon along and had an early curfew. Now a fourteen-year-old goes out without a chaperon and often without a curfew as well. Human nature doesn't change. Our grandparents, or our ancestors three hundred years ago, had the same feelings that we do today. Men and women have always had the same attraction toward one another. Our ideas, our loves, our hates, our passions are the same as they have always been. So really, *we* haven't changed, *but the times we live in have changed.* So just because some of you were not told about the facts of life, or were told too late, please, if you love your children, remember that you must educate them about these facts early and adequately — much earlier probably than you were, and in much more detail than you were, or you run the risk of tragic consequences for your children.

Sex-saturated World

We live in a sex-saturated world. Read the movie ads in the newspaper: "How I Lived As Eve" (rated R), "Magnificent Sinner," "We Weren't Married," etc., and look at the pictures on the page exposing women's and men's bodies in one provocative form or another. On television, radio, billboards, and in newspapers, magazines, and books we are continually reminded of sex. Apparently even drain cleaner can't be sold without some curvaceous blonde pouring it into the sink. You can't turn around today without sex in some form or another being thrown at you. And what is this incessant message we are getting about sex? Simply this—*Sex is fun!* It is something desirable, the end-all and the be-all of living, something that doesn't necessarily have any relation to marriage or love, but something that is desire and want, satisfaction and gratification, and it is more important than anything else. A very selfish picture indeed! Our children can't miss all of this — they listen, watch, read, and too early develop some very warped ideas unless we educate them first. The poignant story of the fifteen-year-old girl at a home for unwed mothers who said, "I grew up to think that if I wore the right designer jeans, happiness would be mine," tragically illustrates our problem.

They Must Be Told

So *you* must tell your children about the facts of life. You *must* tell them. You must *not* be deluded and wait. Too many of us do wait. In our country the average child learns the facts of sexual intercourse from his parents five years after he has heard about them outside the home. The average parent in our country is five years too late! How many children actually find out these truths for the first time from their parents? One child in ten! Nine out of ten learn first on the street, from TV, movies, magazines — in the wrong place, in the wrong way, at the wrong time, from the wrong person, and usually incorrectly. Shocking? This is why we have written this book — to urge you and help you to do the best for your children.

Ignorance or Innocence?

Don't mix up innocence with ignorance. "Oh, she's such a sweet little innocent thing; don't disturb her little world." Ridiculous! There is no relation between innocence and ignorance. Innocence means being pure of heart and free from wrongdoing. Ignorance is lack of information or false information.

Not long ago a principal from a good suburban school called and asked us to speak to his PTA. "I'm not going through another summer like last year — two of our seventh-grade girls got pregnant."

This, we suggest, is plain ignorance of a tragic kind, and can in no way be related to the "innocence" that some parents with their heads in the sand would use as an excuse for not facing the need of educating their children.

If we want to preserve our children's innocence, we must tell them — tell them early — tell them enough.

First Impressions

First impressions are lasting impressions. If children learn about sex first from the street, you may have a very difficult time correcting the warped attitude that may have been shaped in their minds by their first impressions. Each of you take just a second and think. "How, when, where, by whom, and with whom did I first find out and fully realize what sexual intercourse meant and that my parents were doing this together?" Is this a memory that you are pleased with? Do you recall feeling a warm glow within you? You were surprised, yes, but also felt a sense of awe and wonder to know that this was the way that God had given your parents to say to each other in this complete way, "I love you."

Or was your reaction something of dirtiness, distaste, disgust, or guilt? Did you look at your parents or other married couples for days thereafter with an uneasy feeling inside and an unspoken, "Do they do that?" And did you somehow think less of them because of it? Just remember, first impressions of sex can and do color and influence your opinion of sex for the rest of your life. If you love your children, you must tell them first.

Who Tells?

Now for a key question. What do you think is your primary or first duty as parents? Have you ever stopped to think what your most important job is in relation to your children? To feed them? To house them? To clothe them? Yes, these basic necessities must be met, but your most important responsibility is to *educate* them. This is the purpose of marriage: to bring them into the world *and* to educate them — said in the same breath and with equal emphasis. So our work is to be teachers of our children in the broadest sense, which includes the important matters of life and love.

Stop for a minute and consider — "Would I neglect to have my child vaccinated against tetanus?" It would be a rare parent who would fail in this essential care of a youngster. It is usually the other way around — over-anxious mothers rushing the children to the doctor to be sure that they get all the protection they can. And why all this concern? Their physical health is at stake. What about their spiritual and mental health?

Have you vaccinated your child early against the filth and distorted stories he will hear by telling him about this wonderful gift that God has given us parents in cooperating with Him to create new life? This protection is far more important than a tetanus vaccination because it concerns the health of their minds and souls. We parents sincerely want to do the best we can for our children but too often neglect to give this essential information early enough.

From Parents' Lips

This marvelous story of God's love for us comes ideally from your lips, and more importantly from your attitudes. However, many of us develop a mental block and feel most inadequate in explaining matters of sex to our children. A wise college professor once told us, "All mothers hesitate to answer questions related to sex, but if they can just answer their child's first question they are on their way." So prepare yourselves. After your first baby has arrived and you are back to vacuuming the rug, under the protection of the noise from the sweeper's motor, make a habit of saying to yourself, "Babies come out of mommy's womb. Babies come out of mommy's womb." You simply practice, so that when your toddler asks the first question, without batting an eye, stammering, blushing, or getting all flustered, you just say, "Babies come out of mommy's womb," and go right on with your work. If you get over that first hurdle without getting all upset and muttering, "Oh, go ask your Dad" (he doesn't want to answer the question either!), you will be started, and the next questions will be easier.

Let the School Tell Them?

"Oh, the school will do that for us. Wait till then and they'll learn all they need to know." Famous last words! By then it is too late! Do you expect the school to teach your child how to wash his hands, or to feed or dress himself? This basic knowledge he already has when he starts school. The same thing is true about sex — the fundamentals are learned in the home. The idea that mother and daddy love each other and that through their love they bring children into the world is precious knowledge they should already have when they start school. The understanding of this marvelous story of love and God and parents comes from you as parents in a very personal and effective way because of the bond of love you have with your child. This can never be given in the same loving way in an impersonal classroom. It must be done on a person-to-person basis, sensing the need of each individual child — and how differently each one does react! One will say to you, "Oh, Mother, isn't that wonderful!" and another will say, "Yep, uh huh, OK, can I go now?" This is why it is necessary that you tell your own child. They just don't all have the same needs or understand things in the same way. If the school must teach this to your child, it is only because you as parents have failed to do so. These are cold, clinical facts when presented in a classroom or in an educational film and can never convey the true meaning of love. Love is an action, an attitude, a way of life seen and absorbed by a child in his home. Words and pictures in a classroom are an inadequate substitute. The ideal role for the school is to supplement and reinforce the knowledge and attitudes that they have already learned at home. You do want the best for them, don't you?

Why Don't We Tell?

Let's consider for a minute why so many of us don't tell our children about sex. You all know one reason why we don't tell. We feel uncomfortable. But why do we feel this way when we talk to our children about sex? First of all, we are adults, men and women, and we have within us this God-given attraction for one another. It is completely natural and normal for us. When we talk about the weather or baseball or the astronauts, we are on one level of thought and emotion. But the minute sex enters the picture something is a little different, isn't it? We perk up just a little more, we listen a little more keenly, and our blood pressure goes up several points. It's a little different because our adult emotions become involved in this. This is why we may be uncomfortable when our child asks these questions. We are liable to start stammering, blush, or show embarrassment. But remember, the child doesn't have this reaction at all. For a child the questions, "Where do babies come from?" or "How do they get in there?" or "What's for dinner, Mom?" are all on about the same emotional plane — and "What's for dinner" is probably the most important! So we must try to answer these questions with that same flat emotional sameness that the kids ask them. Answer only what is asked. Answer without embarrassment, simply, honestly, and briefly, and go on with what you are doing. If we make a point of letting them know that this is not like talking about other things, they will take notice, become more curious, and get the message, "This is different!"

What If You Haven't Told?

When the children are little their questions are simple, easy, honest, and straight to the point. But what if you have avoided their questions or haven't given them the whole story, and they are already in their middle or late grade-school years? Or what if they are entering their pre-teens and they haven't asked you and you haven't told them? Do you go on blissfully thinking, "Oh, isn't this wonderful — the innocent little things?" Definitely not! If they haven't asked questions by this time, it is your duty to set the stage and talk about it. You must introduce the subject. Children in mid grade school, and girls earlier than boys, are starting to talk about sex with their classmates and playmates, and they're watching TV, reading newspapers, books, and going to movies. They hear and read words like birth control, abortion, rape, homosexual, contraception, etc., which stimulate their curiosity about matters of sex. They wonder about these things, and if you have avoided discussing sex they begin to look at you and wonder why you haven't discussed it. They won't know that the actual reason is your embarrassment. They will think you are not talking about these things because there is something wrong, bad, or dirty about everything relating to sex. They will wonder if you have some guilt that you are hiding. "Why don't mother and dad talk about this? Are they ashamed of this part of their life? At the very least, they can't be very proud of it. Are they doing something bad?" And your children in their grammar-school years will begin to form a definite unhealthy and warped attitude toward sex *because* of your silence.

2

How-to-Tell Techniques

Hesitant?

Even though we parents know the facts for sex instruction, we still hesitate, we still keep back-pedaling. It's like going to the dentist. We know what's going to happen, but we don't like to go. However, we do face up to the dentist — it's part of life — it has to be done — and we proceed. The same is true in giving this most important information about sex to our children. We have to face this, too. It's part of life, of our job as parents. Of even greater importance than "the facts" are our attitudes when we explain these facts to them. Let us first consider some ideas that may help you to introduce the story of sex to your children when they are still very small.

Gradual — Simple

The information is given *gradually,* starting when they are toddlers, and it is added to continuously until they are adults. You don't just take them aside on a sunny afternoon when your boy or girl is about twelve and tell them the whole story. None of that. That just isn't how life operates. They will probably start when they are three or four asking questions like, "Where do babies come from, Mom?" And that is *all* they want to know! A little child's attention span may be thirty

25

seconds—for adults it may be hours if the topic is sex. The
children don't want a postgraduate course—just an on-the-
spot answer—just the facts, Ma'm! The rule with little children is to give as *simple* an answer as you can. If they want
more, let them ask a second question. Give them just as little
information as seems necessary and build on it in the months
and years ahead. Too much detail too early just confuses
them. It is like the story of the small boy who approached
his dad with the question, "Say, Dad, where did I come from?"
The conscientious father braced himself, led the boy into a
private room, and with great care outlined all the details of
the facts of life. After he had finished and was literally wiping
his brow, he asked his son if he had any more questions.
Little Johnny answered brightly, "Yeah, Dad, I just wanted to
know because Joe next door said he came from Chicago and
I was wondering where I came from!"

Do You Know Enough?

Which of you mothers knows the complete mechanics about
blasting a man into space? And yet when your little guy asks,
"Mother, how do they get that man into space?" how many
of you say, "Well Honey, I'll have to get the book out and
look it up" or "Wait till your daddy gets home." Heavens no!
You just dive in and tell the child whatever you know. You
tell him about the big countdown, the rockets blasting off,
the TV monitor, etc. You really don't know much about it, but
you give him a start and know that he will learn a great deal
more in the future. It's the same in answering his questions
about life and love, and the way God has made us. And it has
to be just as spontaneous an answer without stumbling or
hesitating. After all, you do know the facts, you have lived
this life, you can talk about it. Your answer should be given
on the spot, briefly, honestly, and directly, no matter who

may be listening. As many of you know, their questions often come at mealtime or in front of guests!

Call a Spade a Spade

Use correct anatomical terms from the beginning. Just as you call an elbow an elbow and a shoulder a shoulder and don't make up little pet family names for them, do the same when speaking of the breast, the penis, the nipple, etc. Whatever the part of the body is, use its correct name. As the children grow, you need the correct vocabulary to talk to them in order to teach them properly. If you are not sure of them yourself, look them up and practice saying them. Very young children learn words like alligator, bazooka, and dinosaur, and are equally capable of learning the correct body terms.

Do keep a reasonable balance, however. The baby does not grow in mom's "tummy" (that's where the peas and carrots go). But should we use the cold, clinical term "uterus"? We can and should at times, but the word "womb" is softer, accurate, and conveys the message of love and nurturing that you may want. Could you imagine telling your children that a new one is coming by saying, "My dears, I have a fetus growing in my uterus"? No, we presume "baby in my womb" says it better.

The same is true for any bodily function. Whatever says it correctly and doesn't hide it — use it! You don't invent other words for "crying," or for "chewing" — the same applies for "bowel movement," "urinating," or whatever the function is. Use the correct words.

What a boon this would be to a busy doctor when examining children! Imagine one of us asking a four-year-old child about "painful urination." We may have to resort to such phrases as "wee wee," "tinkle," "make a river," and often in desperation, "Does it hurt to pee?"

Kindergarten and first-grade teachers would be greatly helped, too. A first-grade teacher recently had a little girl who wanted to "go to the cafeteria." She presumed her mother was on lunchroom duty, but since it was still an hour until lunch she told her it wasn't time to go. Twice more she came up to her desk to ask to "go to the cafeteria." Finally, the little girl blurted out, "But I just can't wait any longer."

Little People Are Curious

A small child has a great interest in everything around her. Many parents worry when this curiosity extends to the body or bodily functions. They should not, of course, since this is just how preschoolers operate. They are not satisfied to see just one airplane go over; they want to watch dozens and dozens. They just keep observing any and all phenomena over and over. This is part of their education. The same is true in looking at other children at the toilet, in the bathtub, dressing, diaper changing, etc. They just have to keep checking to see what equipment they came with and if everybody else comes with the same parts. This is a normal part of their growing process and is in no way bad. Preschoolers should know that God made boys and girls different. "He made two kinds. Boys have a penis and girls have a vagina. Isn't that nice?" Sleeping, dressing, and bathing little boys and girls together is an acceptable part of their education and may usually be continued until they are able to bathe themselves.

Should They See Our Bodies?

Preschoolers will also be curious about adult bodies and how they differ from their own. Within certain limits they may see you undressed, but let's set some boundaries here. First of all, parents should never give their children the impression that they are ashamed of their bodies. If the little one asks why you cover certain parts with clothes, it is because these are "special parts." If they see you exposed, while dressing, or in the bathroom, you should act relaxed and natural but should, as soon as possible, cover yourself again.

We know that certain differing opinions exist, but few would dispute the fact that little girls should see very little of dad's penis, as this (along with observing actual intercourse, of course) can be very damaging to the psychological formation of a little girl. We would disagree with the "liberal" attitude of certain parents who parade around naked in front of their children, considering it "part of their education." This type of blatant "seductive" exposure is a far cry from the natural, reverent, occasional exposure that occurs at times in families.

For children of any age to see mothers nursing a baby, or to see parents kiss and hug each other, is good. However, children should never see parents petting or becoming involved passionately.

Play with Penis

What about children who play with themselves? If a little boy of preschool age plays with his penis, the parent should act in the same manner as though the child was pulling at his ear or poking a pencil into it. You should simply tell your child, "Mike, stop pulling at your ear or it will get sore," or "Take that pencil out of your ear or you'll hurt it! God made your ear in a very special way and you should take good care of it." You do the same thing if he is playing with his little penis. "Your penis is for passing urine; let it alone and don't rub it or it will get sore." Say this in the same tone of voice you would for any other correction and it will be accepted in the same normal way. The procedure for little girls is similar. Sometimes little girls rub their labia because of skin irritation. The answer then may be simply a bath, a soothing cream, and little overalls.

But, Mommy, It Tickles!

It is best to recognize that preschool children can experience some kind of infantile sex pleasure by rubbing themselves. It is important to know that in young children no guilt should ever be attached to this type of self-play. You can and should simply give a child more attention, ignore a little of it, perhaps distract the child by dressing him, sending him out to play, etc. If, however, the child is doing a lot of this self-play and it is preoccupying his or her time, he or she may need some professional help and it should be obtained. The basis for this self-play, or self-love, is often simply a lack of sufficient parental love and security; or it may be a too-frequent rejection and withdrawing of the parents' love, as is seen in the case of some types of punishment.

It is also known that at a certain state children have strong feeling about wanting to marry their daddy or mother, and can actually harbor some jealousy toward their rival. For example, a little girl resents somewhat the fact that dad shows affection for mother. Ordinarily parents do not worry about these things or understand the psychology of all of this. All that is necessary is just to be natural, loving parents.

These early sexual ideas and feelings of small children are a natural phase in their growing up. In the normal child they fade from consciousness at about the time he or she starts school. Usually children then enter a quiescent phase during the ages of approximately six to eleven years, during which they are usually quite unconcerned about anything of this nature. The reawakening, of course, comes in the early adolescent years unless it has been abnormally stimulated by too much sexual emphases seen and heard on TV, at movies, and in magazines.

The First Questions

Preschoolers ask dozens of questions about everything, and sex is no exception. If your first answers are, "Oh, I'm too busy," or "Don't ask questions like that," or worse yet, "Don't talk about those nasty things," then the next question that occurs to them may not be asked of you. Instead, they will probably ask one of their friends and get the information in the wrong way. You should answer on the spot, be direct, but answer only what they ask. Sometimes your answer may be over their heads, as we found out with our four-year-old daughter. She heard us discussing a proper mate for our female dog, Sandy, who was always getting out at the wrong time and mating with the wrong daddy dog. "Why do we have to have a daddy dog?" she queried. "So that the daddy dog can plant the seed in Sandy." She gave that exasperated child look and said, "Oh, Daddy, you know dogs can't plant grass seed." It was more than she could grasp at her age! "Because God made it that way" would probably have been enough at that time.

No Questions from Your Child?

If your child has not asked any of the usual questions and is about ready to start grade school, then you should ask a few questions. "Isn't it nice Aunt Jane's going to have a baby?" "Uh huh." "Did you ever wonder where babies come from?" "Huh uh." With a little perseverance you can find out what they know or don't know and give them the information you want them to have. Even if the child doesn't seem interested, a few comments as to the baby growing in mother's womb, etc., should be made.

Be Honest

There is also another problem that a hesitant mother may have created by making up stories. One common one likens the hospital to a supermarket where the mother walks up and down the aisle and picks out the very baby she wants. If you have been telling a story like this, you had better straighten it out today because if your child finds out that you are lying to him about this, then he will not trust you on future answers. This trust in you is particularly important later as he or she gets into the preteens and teens. You will not then want earlier mistakes to have destroyed this confidence in you. For heaven's sake, be honest. If you have been making up stories, or perhaps by mistake have told him something that isn't quite true, then say, "Up until now, Donny, I didn't think you were old enough to know certain things, but now that you're old enough I want to explain these things to you."

And square with him!

Modesty

By the time children start grade school, the idea that God made their bodies and that they are something special should be understood. With a little encouragement children should develop a respect and reverence for their bodies and a growing consciousness of modesty. This tends to develop earlier and be more marked in girls than in boys. Prudishness should be avoided, but their right to privacy should be respected. By teaching them to keep the special parts of their bodies covered and never to expose them or allow another person to touch them, you are also protecting them from possible harm by a sexual pervert.

Adoption

How do these ideas apply if your child is adopted? Probably no flat, universally applicable rules can be set down because age and conditions vary so much, but let's try.

In general, the story of sex and creation as spoken of throughout this book should be taught the very same way to your adopted children as to your biologically natural children, just as your love for them and attitudes toward them should be no different than for natural children.

They must know they are adopted and grow up with this knowledge. There are few exceptions to this. It is far easier to grow into this than to be told in young adulthood; and think of the impact if they learn about it from others.

The inevitable questions about their true parents are answered differently at different ages. Several ideas are woven into your answers to this question: ... You do not know who they are and it is impossible to find out. ... You do not even know if they are alive.... They must have been good people who knew they could not properly raise her and gave her up so she would have two parents and a good home (The older child who knows about the possibility of abortion will understand if you tell her that her mother was a good person — she carried and delivered her, then gave her up).... You, of course, picked her out especially. Finally, you ask her, what does all of the above matter? What really counts is that you love her, you wanted her, worked hard to get her, and in every way but one are actually and completely her parents.

Love Again

The most important theme running through all of this education is your own attitude. It is not so much *what* you tell your children as *how* you tell them and *how you live*. If you show them that mother and daddy love each other, that this is how God intended it to be, and that at times He blesses this love with children, then you have given them something no one else can give your child.

Your children will usually grow up to live as you have *shown* them, as you yourselves have lived and loved, not as they have been *told* to live. If your home has been a happy, loving, generous, secure nest, then the little people God has given you will become a credit to you and will be able to create similar loving homes themselves someday. The greatest teaching is in the minute-to-minute, day-to-day living of your lives with them as they absorb attitudes, opinions, ways of acting, selfishness or unselfishness, loving neighbors or hating them, prejudice, fair play, pride, tolerance of others, right or wrong, self-discipline or self-indulgence, respect for authority, and on and on through the myriad of ideas and attitudes that you bequeath to them — most often unthinkingly.

Teach By Example

An old story may help us. It seems that Grandpa was quite old and feeble and always spilt coffee on the table. To remedy this inconvenience he was banished to a small side table and given a wooden cup. (This was in the days before plastic.) One day little Johnny was busying himself whittling on a piece of wood. "What are you doing, Johnny?" asked his mother. "Oh, I didn't have anything to do today and I thought I'd make two wooden cups — one for you and one for Dad. You see, some day when I'm big and you and Dad are old, I'll need two cups for you when we put you at the side table."

We do teach, don't we?

3

How to Answer the Questions

Beginning

In the first few weeks and months of your infant's life, you teach a great deal by your actions whether you realize it or not. In the way you handle your little one, and love him, and answer his cries and so on, you are teaching him a great deal about love and trust for another person. The normal matter-of-factness with which you bathe him, change his diaper, feed, and dress him show him very clearly that all bodily care and functions are necessary, normal, and not bad. Toilet training later should be handled in the same way with some praise (but not bribery) for his efforts to cooperate, but never, never punishment for failure. It is just part of growing up. It is now known that the nervous system which controls the bladder and bowel functions matures at different ages in different children and that some children do not develop conscious daytime control of bladder and bowels until they reach age three or even later. Most parents are now aware of the fact that forcing a child to bowel and bladder train too early can be harmful psychologically. You must gently but firmly resist the occasional well-intentioned grandmother who would force this too soon, as her generation often mistakenly did.

The First Question

As the child reaches the age of three, four, or five she becomes more aware of others and begins to voice those first inquiring ideas, and then one day says, "Mommy, where do babies come from?" You simply answer, "Out of mommy's womb. The baby grows there under her heart where it is safe and warm." Maybe she'll say, "Why?" "This is how God made it." For the very small ones, this is all they may really want to know. The same questions will probably be asked again and each time should be answered with the same matter-of-factness.

New Baby

If you are expecting a new baby, tell them ahead of time and let them feel the little baby kick in your womb. The joy of expecting a new baby that you show during these pregnant months is also a powerful teacher, not by words, but by attitude toward this new life growing within you. Remember, you can also implant an unhealthy attitude toward pregnancy in your child's mind if you constantly complain about your "condition," feel sorry for yourself, and are too tired and too irritable to show love for anyone. This could teach children very effectively that a mother should be sick during pregnancy, that perhaps they were not really wanted either, and that somehow it is dad's fault. This early training might contribute toward forming the child into a selfish, frigid woman who fears pregnancy and who in general rejects her true feminine role in life, as some women tragically do.

Occasionally, of course, a woman is actually physically sick because of, or during, her pregnancy. In this case, the children must be told that this is not normally so, but that pregnancy is a normal function of the mother's body. Even in the presence of physical problems, however, the mother should still have a happy and healthy emotional attitude toward her pregnancy and the anticipated little one.

Next Questions

The next question may be, "Mommy, how does the baby get out?" — "When the baby is big enough to live outside of mother's body, she goes to the hospital and the doctor helps the baby come out." "Where does the baby come out?" "There's a special opening between mother's legs, and the doctor helps the little baby come out from there."

If the question comes, "How big is that opening?" you could say, "Well, Johnny, you know what a balloon is. If we blow it up it gets big, and then when you let the air out it gets small again. That's how it is with mother's opening. It gets big to let the baby out and then gets small again." — "Let me see it!" — (steady now!) — "No, Johnny, that's one of the special parts of mother's body that she doesn't show to anyone."

If not now, at some time later you may be faced with, "Does it hurt when the baby comes out?" Don't say, "Oh, it's awful!" But rather, "Oh, it hurts some, but the doctor gives you medicine and the nurse is there to take care of you, and after the baby comes you are just so happy to have a new little baby to bring home that you forget all about it. It is just so wonderful to have a new baby to love." Again, you are emphasizing the love and the goodness of it.

Another early question frequently will be, "How does the baby start?" or "How does the baby get in there?" For the very young child the following answer is usually sufficient: "When God wants to send Mother and Daddy a new child the baby starts to grow in mommy's womb." Later on, the child may ask, "But how does it get in there?" "Daddy plants a seed in mother's body which joins with her egg and grows into a new baby." This may be sufficient for the time, or there may be another question immediately, "Well, how does Daddy plant the seed?"

How Does Daddy Plant the Seed?

By this time the child is probably in early grade school years or maybe middle grade school years. "You know how Mother and Daddy love each other?" "Yes." Because they have seen you hugging and kissing and showing your love for each other. "You know how Mother and Daddy hug and kiss?" "Uh huh." "Well, some night when Mother and Daddy love each other especially much, some seeds from Daddy's body go into Mother's body, and, if God wills, a new baby starts to grow. You see, Mother, Dad, and God are all needed to bring a baby into the world. . . . That's how you came. Isn't that wonderful?"

When your child is somewhat older, your answer is more detailed. "Some night when Mother and Daddy are loving each other very much (this is the clue, when you are loving each other and expressing your love for each other), Daddy's penis goes into Mother's vagina and the seed from Daddy is planted where it may join the egg in Mother's body, and, if God wills, a new baby starts to grow." Again you've told them very fundamental things without any extras. In these early years they need only the basic ideas. "God surely must love us to have everything worked out so well." "Gee, Mom, I sure think so, too," or some similar indication of wonder or awe may follow to show how this information is received by your child. The question of pleasure in the marital act usually does not occur to the child at this time, but if it does your answer could be, "Yes, it's enjoyable, just like Mother and Daddy like to kiss and hug." More elaboration on this subject will come when you are talking with your child when he or she is older.

Newspaper Stories

Give them a chance to sound you out on articles they have read in the newspaper with words like "abortion," "rape," "unwed mother," etc. Any child who watches TV, goes to movies, or reads magazines or newspapers sees these words, and stores them up to get the explanation either from you or from someone else. It is far better to tell your children the meaning of these words than to risk them getting it incorrectly from outside your home. Give them the simplest answers possible, knowing that you will add to their information in the future.

For Example — Rape

A good opportunity for a preteen or teen-age daughter to have uninterrupted time with her mother is on her night for helping mom in the kitchen. (No other member of the family is usually in sight — until every dish is done!) You could say to your girl, "Wasn't it sad reading about that little girl being raped? Sally, do you understand what they mean by rape?" "Well, uh — kinda — but not real well, I guess." Then in the words that come best to you answer her along these lines. "Sally, unfortunately not all people are good in this world. Some rob banks, others drive cars at ridiculous speeds and end up killing or injuring others, etc. And so it is with sexual actions. God loved us enough to give us a free will and we can either say 'yes' or 'no' to the way He wants us to live. He gave married people this wonderful way of showing their love for each other in the joining of their bodies in sexual intercourse. Now some people want to do this outside of marriage. Rape is when a man forces a girl or woman to whom he is not married to have sexual relations with him when she doesn't want to. He is being very selfish and thinking of only what he wants." "Mom, that's awful." "Yes it is, dear, and that's why we don't want you to come home alone at night."

"And What Is Abortion?"

"And what is abortion, Mother?" "Sally, you know how the baby grows and develops in the mother's womb?" "Yes." "Some mothers don't want a new baby after it starts growing in their bodies, so they have an operation performed that kills the baby in their womb. As we know, only God can create that life and only He has the right to take that life away. Killing an unborn child is a terrible thing." "But, Mother, why wouldn't a mother want her own child?" "Again, Sally, we can't judge other people's motives, but it is usually based on selfish reasons — 'What I want' — 'my convenience' — 'my comfort.' As you grow older you will realize that it is not always easy to do the right thing." "OK, Mom, thanks." "Anytime, Sally. If you don't understand things like this, please ask me."

Girls Mature Before Boys

Changes preparing a young girl for womanhood usually begin taking place about nine, ten, or eleven years of age, while boys mature two or three years later. The first girl in a class who menstruates may be as young as eight or nine years old. This seems quite young, and, as a matter of fact, girls do menstruate on the average of a year or two earlier than they did fifty years ago. This means that you should tell your daughter about her approaching womanhood by the time she is eight, or at least nine. She should know about menstruation by the time the first one in her class or in her group begins to menstruate. Girls pass this information along to their friends, and if you have not explained this to your daughter she will be wondering why her mother has not said anything to her.

Menstruation — The First Telling

The first time you mention menstruation make it simple and brief; since she has not experienced this yet, she will not remember details. At this stage she needs to know only the simple facts so that when it happens to her, she will not be shocked, bewildered, or frightened. Tell her merely — "You will soon be growing into a young lady. When you have grown enough you will begin to have a bloody discharge from your vagina about once a month. This is called menstruation and you'll have to wear either a Kotex or a tampon (and explain what they are). We'll talk about the details later when your body begins to change, or anytime you have any questions."

Menstruation — Later Details

Your later explanation will probably go something like this: "Jane, your body is changing and you are growing up. You are no longer a 'little kid.' It's wonderful to be growing up and becoming a young lady. God has built within your body and every woman's body the tremendous potential of having babies. It is a marvelous thing to think that some day you could grow up and become a mother. In order that this can happen some day, you have special organs in your body that are called female organs. These organs are the womb or uterus, tubes, ovaries, and vagina, and are located in your pelvis, which is in the lower part of your abdomen. The womb is a hollow, pear-shaped organ which serves as the nest in which the baby grows for nine months inside its mother.

"There are two small tubes which open out from the womb on either side. Through these tubes the eggs pass from the ovaries, which are small almond-shaped structures located at the ends of the tubes. An egg is usually released once every month from an ovary and begins its passage through the tube into the womb. If the seed (sperm) from the father joins the seed (egg or ovum) from the mother, a new baby will begin to develop in her womb. If the tiny developing baby is not planted in the womb, then the womb passes off the food and nourishment stored in its lining that would have been used to nourish the baby. This monthly passage of a watery-bloody discharge is called menstruation and lasts three to seven days and occurs about once a month. This menstrual flow passes through the vagina, which is a tube connecting the lower part of the womb to the external opening, the vaginal opening, and during this time a Kotex or a tampon is worn to catch the flow. This cycle works like perfect clockwork with no one having to wind or tend the clock."

Then remember to question her so that you are sure she understands at least the basic ideas.

Menstruation Is Normal

It is an absolutely normal process so avoid phrases like "the curse" or "monthly sickness," etc. It is as normal as urinating. The attitudes you give your daughter she will carry with her for life. When a girl first starts to menstruate there are usually no cramps, so do not worry her about them at this time. Show her what Kotex, belts, and tampons are and emphasize the special care she should take of her body, which has been made for such great things. Encourage her to come to you with any future problems or questions. When mother and daughter share life's deeper ideas of creation and love, the bond of trust and confidence between them is strengthened.

After you have told your daughter about the basic facts, and she is about ready to or has begun to menstruate, then you may give her a simple book to read about menstruation.

Movie on Menstruation?

What about showing the girls a movie on menstruation? Excellent! For seventh or eighth graders. Some groups are showing detailed films on this subject to children in the fourth and fifth grades, and we must disagree. Our suggestion would be that this impersonal presentation of facts in such great detail to young children is simply too much too early. These films would be very usefully shown to the *mothers* of the fourth-or fifth-grade girls to prepare them better to tell their daughters. Ideally we do not think these should be shown to the girls themselves until after they have already been told by their mothers and some have experienced menstruation personally. It is not until about seventh or eighth grade that many of the girls actually have begun to menstruate. This overanxiousness to teach the little girls detailed clinical facts about menstruation in large public groups is a mistake that modern mothers seem to have fallen into unaware and with the best of intentions. A simple question may help to put this in proper perspective. "Are you showing movies on the detailed functioning of the digestive system in the fourth and fifth grades?" "No — too early." Right. Too early also, then, for a detailed movie on menstruation at this age. Let little children be. Encourage their mothers to give them sketchy outlines of how their bodies will function. The complete facts should come later when they are about to begin or after they have begun to menstruate and can apply the information to themselves.

Let Susie's Mother Tell Her

One word of warning to your daughter at this time: "Now Sue's mother will want to tell her the things I'm telling you so you won't need to tell her." This is particularly true for girls because they tend to talk more, and are eager to pass on information. If there is no mother in the home and no aunt or close friend to establish this confidence with the child — or if the mother would be incapable because of insufficient mental ability, alcoholism, etc. — then a teacher could be a mother substitute in giving these early basic facts.

Who Tells the Boy?

It is most important for a father to tell his son about the masculine changes that will occur in him. It is generally not for a mother to explain to her boy the facts about his oncoming manhood. If, unfortunately, there is no father in the home, it is better for an uncle or some close adult male friend (a father figure) to tell this story to the boy. This man-to-man talk is perhaps initiated when a boy is about eleven, twelve, or thirteen, since boys mature about two or three years later than girls. Except for muscles and physical strength, boys are generally less interested in their bodies, and certainly talk less about social-sexual aspects of maturing than girls do at this age. Yet when a boy does begin to mature, he can talk too. There will probably be some showoff to tell your boy how to masturbate and/or what to do with girls. It is important for the father to go into some real detail before the above has happened and, for the first time, to have a private man-to-man talk.

Man to Man

Your (the father's) telling it will be effective because it is from you and because of your sincerity and authority, even if not technically accurate in every detail. Perhaps you would start thus: "Jim, you are growing up and soon will be a young man. Your body is starting to change and perhaps we'd better have a little talk about all of this." And then you tell him what the changes are. His penis is getting longer, his scrotal sack is lengthening, he is having erections, etc.

Wet Dreams

Explain that soon male seeds or sperm will begin to be formed in his testicles. "If you marry, this is the seed that you'll put in your wife's body. There is no need for this seed yet and so your body will store it and occasionally release the overflow at night while you are sleeping. This is what we call a wet dream or nocturnal emission. Usually you will have a rather vivid dream which culminates in a very pleasant feeling in your penis. You will wake up with sticky wet pajamas from some milky, mucous-like material that has come from your penis." Reassure him that this is quite normal, and is not wrong in any way.

Masturbation

As the boy grows, there should be more discussion about these things between father and son, exploring the progressing physical and emotional changes that are occurring.

When the time seems opportune, face up to the fact that in the early teens most boys begin to masturbate. This again is not for mother to talk about—it is for dad. It is often extremely difficult for dad to face this, the reason being that quite frequently dad may carry with him some guilt feelings from his youth about masturbation. However, this discussion is important, and no one can speak as effectively about it as a boy's own dad. You should explain that his sex powers have a specific purpose and are not to be misused. The strong, mature man will learn to reserve these powers as his gift to his wife when he marries.

A Helpful Example

As an aid in impressing the sanctity of sex upon a boy (or a girl) you might use this example in talking to your child.

"Now, Jim, let's say that a young man and a young lady who aren't married would go to a motel together. He would kiss her, touch her breasts, and then go all the way, and have sexual intercourse with her. What would you think?" "That would be wrong, Dad! They aren't allowed to do that." "All right, now let's suppose that this same young man and lady would marry each other and then on their honeymoon go through the very same actions together again, what then?" "Well, now it would be OK because they're married and they are allowed to do that." "More than that, Jim, the same actions that were wrong before marriage now become not just permitted, but good. We believe that these marriage acts, when used as an expression of love for one's partner, while wrong before marriage, become positively good and sacred in marriage. And remember, Jim, this doesn't apply only to the complete sex act; it also applies to the preliminary actions of petting that are a preparation for intercourse. These intimate actions will be made sacred in marriage, too, and shouldn't be misused or given cheaply to each other before marriage."

When Dating Begins

We would hope that double dating would not begin before about the junior year of high school. (See Chapters 6 to 13.) Further frank discussion should then be added to what has already been said. Often at this time it is good for both parents to talk to the child. This is always personal between parent and child. Its timing depends on the maturity of the boy or girl, on the prevailing dating customs, etc. Let us briefly indicate some areas to be discussed, particularly . . .

For Girls

She must be specifically told that her virtue is in her own hands. "It is the girl who sets the limits if the boy won't." Furthermore, with few exceptions, even "good" boys will take liberties if sufficiently tempted and permitted to do so by the girl. Give her the full responsibility. Tell her that her body is worth exactly the value she places on it. If she gives it cheaply, cheap it is.

It is up to the girl not to provide temptation. Explain to her that an embrace, for instance, may be for her just a pleasant feeling of being wanted. However, the same embrace for the boy may be cause for deep sexual arousal. What for her is just being popular may be a strong sexual stimulus to him. Discuss with her what tight sweaters, short shorts, stretch pants, tight jeans, and the like may do to a boy.

For Boys

Tell him that he is the leader and should control what happens on a date. Encourage him to be polite, chivalrous, and respectful of his girl friend. Explain to him that it is the weak man who is just out for a thrill, and that it is the strong man, the real man, who can control himself. Give him all the responsibility.

Petting

Everyone interprets this word differently. If you use it in your talking, best to tell them what you mean by it. Petting means that one of them touches the private parts of the other's body with his (her) hands. This definitely includes her breasts, clothed or otherwise. By traditional Judeo-Christian moral standards, petting is preparation for intercourse and to pet outside of marriage is a serious wrong.

Also tell them about . . .

Love

Love is more than passion and sex (see Chapter 5). It is doing good for your loved one, wanting the best for your loved one. It is giving of your effort, thoughts, and time freely to your loved one for her (his) happiness, well-being, and spiritual good without necessarily expecting anything in return.

Let's look in the back seat of a car and see a young unmarried couple. He declares his love for her — a love apparently so great that he asks her to give him privileges with her body. This song is as old as humanity and your children will be hearing it. Tell your dating children this story and then look at it a bit closer. Ask them, does he really love her? Is this real love? Does he want the best for her? Is this a true concern for the well-being and happiness of his "loved one"? Does he love her? — or only himself? Does he really want only her body? We'll return to this couple later after we examine love and sex a little closer. Meanwhile, let's remember that . . .

When "love" becomes self-centered, selfish, a taking rather than a giving, it ceases to be love at all. Love is nothing if it is not a free gift, given to make the loved one a better, happier, more secure, contented, and holier person. Love expects nothing for the giver except the happiness of the one loved.

Let's look closer at our attitudes about sex . . .

4

Attitudes

Our Mixed-up Heritage on Sex Attitudes

We cannot give what we haven't got. If our attitudes toward sex are warped, incomplete, or incorrect, we tend to pass this on to our children. Many of us come from a mixed-up heritage as far as sex is concerned. We older adults were born into a world where the attitude toward sex had been formed by a prudish Victorian mentality. The Victorian Age taught that sex was something we didn't talk about. Sex was something to be kept hidden, something merely permitted in marriage, something to turn the lights out for, something never discussed by "nice" people. These attitudes are still deeply ingrained in many people's thinking. Contrast this with our current sex-saturated age. Complete sexual freedom is widely accepted today by women as well as men — freedom to talk and act as one pleases about sex, denial of sin and of moral good or evil, complete liberty, or libertarian license for anybody. This mix-up in our culture today between these two extremes has caused great confusion to say the least.

What of sexual morality in the American culture? If we look, we see that a parallel movement has occurred. Protestant Puritanism is matched by Catholic Jansenism, and Catholics have been heir to a tradition typified by the Irish grandmother who felt the same way about sex as her good

Protestant neighbor did. She knew sex was needed for having babies, but to her it was her *duty*, a necessary evil to be tolerated. She might have thought that God did a pretty good job of creating the whole world, but He must have gotten tired late on the sixth day and didn't do too good a job creating the lower parts of our bodies. This attitude was never to our knowledge officially taught by any of the major churches in America, but many people, and sometimes even the clergy, reflected this thinking. "Sex is a concession to man's weakness, and God tolerates it. It is permitted in marriage because, after all, we must continue to have babies and if this is the only method of producing them, we'll have to put up with it." Forgive us if we exaggerate to make our point. Nevertheless this inherited prudish attitude along with current libertarian thinking is the cause of a fantastic amount of sexual maladjustment and marital unhappiness and directly affects the younger generation through their mixed-up parents.

A Wife's Duty

A wife has a duty to her husband? True — but what a twisted connotation is sometimes attached to this. Let us get our thinking straight here. It is our duty to eat to sustain life, certainly. But does this infer a joyless, repetitious chore? Of course not. There is pleasure and satisfaction from eating and we should enjoy our food (as long as we control our appetite and refrain from gluttony and drunkenness). So too with sex.

Sex Is Sacred

We should regard sex with reverence and awe, with pride and gratitude. God could have made babies by growing them

on trees, but He didn't. He chose the way each of us knows.
He chose so to arrange things that a man and woman would
mutually unite their bodies in an act of love (which He would
at times bless with new life). The Book of Genesis tells us,
"God made man. Male and female, He made them." Men and
women are different according to divine plan. Furthermore,
Adam and Eve were told to "increase and multiply and sub-
due the earth." They were created with physical bodies exactly like ours and were given this command to reproduce
themselves (by having intercourse) before their rebellion. This
rebellion brought many consequences, but it did not change
God's plan for men and women to unite their bodies in this
act of love and procreation.

The Old Testament refers again and again to God and His
bride, Israel — Israel, His spouse, who, though often unfaithful
to Him, is always loved by Him and welcomed back to her
Bridegroom when she repents. The New Testament speaks
again in terms of nuptial arrangements, with Christ, the Bridegroom, and the Church, His bride. St. Paul likens the union
of husband and wife with the union of Christ and His Church.
These terms have not been used accidentally. God has blessed
marriage. The act of love that we share in marriage is a
sacred thing. We must realize this. Just think for a moment:
if there were no sin in the world, when would the marital act
be used? It would be used only between a loving husband
and wife, in marriage, to express unselfish love for each
other, to give to each partner joy and happiness, and when
God wills it, a child. Many have abused sex, certainly, but
that does not change its basic goodness any more than the
abuse of alcoholism would make thirst a bad thing.

Who Married You?

The clergyman did not actually marry you. By your official
and solemn pledge together, you married each other, as man

and wife, to have and to hold, for life. The clergyman is the official witness of church and state. Now, were you married at the altar? Well, yes, but not completely. If you two had walked away from each other at that time and had never lived together, your marriage could have been dissolved. It would never have been a complete marriage. Your marriage was a complete marriage only when the two of you, in expressing your love for each other, united your bodies in intercourse. Then, at that moment, you were completely married and the sacred marriage contract fulfilled.

Christians Believe

Most Christians believe that by this very action Christ more fully enters and enriches their lives. Furthermore, theologians tell us that grace descends upon us, enriches our lives, fills our souls, not as a one-time occurrence on the day of marriage, but continuously as a steady stream throughout married life. Each time husband and wife display toward each other the unselfishness of a giving love, whether it be the wife preparing a good meal, or the husband's thoughtful phone call when he finds he will be late for dinner, or whether it is the complete giving of each other in bed, Christ's love and life in them is increased. Christian teaching certainly makes the marriage bed a holy place, but how many individual Christians look upon it this way?

Proud of Sex

You must demonstrate to your children, by the very lives you lead, that all parts of your bodies are good and holy, not just your brain or heart. Your sex organs are holy too. Each part was made for a reason. When you use each part and function of your bodies in the way that God has intended, you are doing His will, being blessed, and in following this plan should find your "fullest measure of earthly happiness."

Pride of Manhood and Womanhood

Each parent should carry great pride in his manhood or in her womanhood. A man should be proud of his masculinity and act like it — be proud of being the protector, breadwinner, and head of the house. A woman should be proud of her femininity and act like it, and as a loving mother and wife be truly the heart of the home whether she is a full-time wife and mother or whether she also works outside the home. Then, almost coming out of the very pores of your skin, this attitude of joy and pride of being a man or a woman will be absorbed by your children. This is the attitude to give your children.

Breasts

There is no better example of this mixed-up attitude toward sex than the glorification of women's breasts in our culture. What does the world think about women's breasts today? It uplifts them, sticks them out, lowcuts the dress around them, and flaunts them in the face of every man as sexually enticing objects. Is this why women have breasts? Only for sex? Isn't this really why you wear a tight sweater and an uplift bra? To make yourself attractive to men? Don't forget that if your twelve- or fifteen-year-old daughter dresses this way, she is making herself sexually provocative to men. Now, let us not lose our proper perspective here. Women do have breasts for a sexual reason. This is a good reason and a healthy one when used properly. It is for feminine attractiveness, to help attract a husband, and to be a source of mutual joy and pleasure to both partners in marriage. However, this is a *secondary* reason. The *primary* reason women have breasts is to feed babies. And yet, while it's apparently all right to use them in a seductive fashion in public, what do people think when a mother nurses a baby in public?

Nurse in Public!

We don't advocate breast-feeding in ball parks or other public places. However, in the presence of family or close friends it is entirely fitting and proper. After all, we enjoy eating with our families and friends, so why should we be ashamed to give an innocent babe the food God has provided for him? This is a totally natural and normal way to feed a baby. Our culture is unique in the entire world in viewing it with such prudishness.

Expose Yourself to Nurse?

Please understand how a modern mother looks when she nurses. Today's clothes are very well designed for a nursing mother to use modestly. There are two-piece dresses, button-down-the-front blouses, "trapdoor" nursing bras, all adaptable to limiting exposure of the breast. The sometimes-seen advertisements that show a nursing mother all but stripped to the waist are totally unrealistic and probably do more to discourage a woman from nursing than to encourage her (and we do mean the companies that sell prepared baby-milk formulas). With modern clothes, you can nurse a baby in the presence of others and they may not even be aware of the fact, thinking rather that you are merely cuddling the babe.

In Front of My Son?

Not long ago I asked a mother in the hospital if she was going to nurse this baby as she had her other ones. She said,

"I don't think I should nurse this one because I now have a teen-age son." I gently chided her, "Mary, this is why you *should* nurse this baby." "But he'd see me," she retorted. "Exactly right and he should! Look, Mary, your boy is going to be dating girls, and he's going to be dancing with girls, and holding them next to him, and feeling their breasts against him. He'll be looking, and wanting to see and feel their breasts. He's getting the message that is being thrown at him. 'Breasts are a plaything, forbidden but fun.' If he sees you nurse, he'll appreciate what breasts are really for. He'll see the maternal love that you give your child by nursing, and he'll gain a great deal more respect for you as a woman, for his girlfriend as a woman, and will be more able to respect her breasts." We must educate our boys and our girls to value their bodies. Remember that an adult man's reaction to observing a nursing mother is almost universally devoid of any sexual stimulation. This madonna image rather stirs within him a softness, warmth, respect, and goodness, and a father realizes more fully his protective guardianship of this loving pair.

Why Nurse

Thank goodness breast-feeding has again become "respectable." A majority of new mothers have reclaimed their birthright and are breast-feeding again. They are seeing the fallacy of the Victorian, feminist rejection of true femininity, and returning to their normal function of being a complete mother. Let us dispel a few misconceptions before we move on:

1. There is no such thing as poor or weak breast milk. You either have enough of it or you don't, but what there is, with rare exceptions, is good milk. When doctors use the words "poor" or "weak," they usually mean that the mother has an insufficient volume or quantity of milk,

and, of course, this is a major reason for being unsuccessful in nursing.

2. Thin, watery-looking breast milk *is* mother's milk, rich and strong. It is not cow's milk and we should not expect it to look like cow's milk.

3. Very small and very large breasts both will produce ample milk for a child. The size of the breasts does not relate to a mother's ability to nurse successfully.

4. You will not lose your figure from nursing. Pregnancy can change the size and shape of breasts, but nursing, with proper supportive bras, will cause no further change.

Advantages

To Mother

1. A mother who has nursed has a smaller chance of developing breast cancer or cysts in the breasts.

2. Nursing, *full-time*, usually prevents ovulation and keeps the mother from menstruating or conceiving another child. This means that the mother gives her baby total nourishment from her breasts and does not give extra milk or other food. This natural method of spacing children, however, often does not work if the baby gets extra bottle milk, cereal, and jar food.

3. The bond of love and unity that a nursing mother should feel with her baby can be an almost indescribable sense of fulfillment and joy in being a complete mother, and is well described by a fond mother who with great warmth looked down at her peacefully nursing son and said, "We're buddies."

4. It's convenient. You don't have to buy milk, prepare formulas, sterilize and warm bottles, etc.

To Baby

1. Well-nursed babies are happier babies.
2. The baby cannot be allergic to his mother's milk. Consequently, breast-fed babies seldom have eczema or other allergy problems which are so frequent with babies fed on formulas, almost all of which are made from cow's milk.
3. There is substantially less colic and digestive upsets are fewer than in bottle-fed babies.
4. They seldom have constipation.
5. Breast-fed babies have less diaper and other skin rashes than bottle-fed babies.
6. They also receive substantial protection from infections through their mother's milk.

To Dad

1. It's cheaper.
2. You don't have to get up at night!
3. You are never more a man and rightfully proud of it than when you see your dependent, beautifully feminine wife and nursing babe, and realize that they are yours to care for, support, and protect—that they need you.

A Secure, Contented Child

A happy mother with a bottle can and often does produce a contented baby, but it seems obvious that good breast-feeding gives a substantially greater chance of producing a happy, contented child. You just cannot give with a glass bottle and rubber nipple the degree of intimacy and security, of sustained and continuous love, or emotional security, that you can achieve with the baby's mouth against your warm breast, and his little ear against your chest listening to your heartbeat. Perhaps you must spend more time with the baby when you nurse. That is the way God made it, and if it takes a little longer to nurse, it is for the very reason that the baby needs you longer. No one else can feed the baby? That's right; the baby needs you, not your mother-in-law, or husband, or baby sitter.

Let us, of course, retain a balanced viewpoint on breast-feeding. Some mothers are unable to nurse no matter how hard they try. However, even a little overemphasis on its values will help correct some of our parents' generation's rejection of it.

Bodies Are Holy

Above all, teach your children the dignity and the true value of their bodies. Remember, out of our Creator's infinite wisdom, our bodies were made just as they are. Our sexual organs and the most exquisite enjoyment that can be obtained by having intercourse is just the way God planned it. All He asks is that these powers be used according to His plan. If so, these actions are good and holy. Sex, in and of itself, is not love. It is only an expression of love, the most complete way of showing love for one's partner. Just as a kiss is an expression of love, a way of saying, "I love you," but not love in and of itself, so with sexual intercourse. Truly, it is the most complete, expressive, and total way of saying, "I love you," but it too is not love itself, but just a way of expressing and showing love. If it is an honest expression, then it must be a generous, permanent, unselfish gift of self to the loved one. If your children get this message from you, their mother and dad, instead of the false siren song of today's hypocritical world, how fortunate they will be!

5

Love

What Is Love?

Many of us are mixed up about love, and certainly most children are! We all talk about love, think about love, and yet we seem to use the word "love" in so many different ways.

Love, to many, usually means sexual love between a man and woman. However, sometimes it seems to be broader than sex. How about an aged wife caring for her sick husband; that's love, too, isn't it? What about a child loving her mother? These would seem to be very different kinds of love, wouldn't they? But let's go further. The Bible tells us to love our neighbor. Does this really mean love, or did they just translate it wrong?

Now let's add to the apparent confusion. How about loving God? Now that certainly can't be the same love as the love of two sweethearts, can it?

We even use the phrase "love to swim" or "I'd love to go to the game." Also, is "I like him" the same, if perhaps a bit less, than "I love him"? How about this business of loving our enemies? Now that really confuses things. Do we all mean something different when we say we love different people? Does religion teach us one kind of love, our own bodies another, our minds another?

Really, we are for the most part quite mixed up on what

love really is. And, goodness knows, if we don't even know what we mean by love, how in the world can we really know if we are in love, or loving, or being loved? How can we teach our children what we don't know? Let's look further . . .

Love Our Neighbor?

"Loving our neighbor." Sounds like religion. A different kind of love, perhaps? Something to be applied if and when we decide to. The condescension of charity given at Christmas, or a donation to the United Way? For most, loving one's neighbor is a very selective affair and we reserve the right to select who, when, and how much. Perhaps a modern rule of thumb would be that this gift of love should never inconvenience us.

Love God

Of course, we all love God, or we are supposed to, or we'd like to. But what does this mean? Well, you know. I pray sometimes, donate to the church, keep most of the commandments most of the time. If I'm Methodist or Mormon, I probably don't drink; if I'm Catholic, I go to Mass on Sundays and keep the other rules of the church. Sure, I love God, but it's pretty hard to love someone you can't see or talk to. Perhaps this love is in a little compartment in one corner of our minds and we pull it out on the Sabbath or Sunday and then put it away the rest of the week. You've heard of whited sepulchers?

Love My Husband or Wife

Or boyfriend? or girlfriend? Oh, now this is different! Especially before marriage. It has something to do with sex, with a great want, a deep yearning to be with, to possess my partner. It is powerful. It is a need to be satisfied, a thrill to be sought, a passion, an enjoyment, a self-satisfaction, a self-gratification. It is romance, too. Moonlight, dreams, beauty, wealth, success, and happiness ever after! Or so Hollywood tells us! The odd thing is that those famous figures of stage and screen, of society and wealth who have all these things, don't very often seem to be happy. In fact, they sometimes die in a drunken coma, or commit suicide to escape the misery of their lives.

And then, we see a very ordinary couple who are not very handsome, smart, or successful, but who are very devoted to each other and who are, strangely enough, happy!

Strange World, Isn't It!

You've heard the quip, "Money doesn't make people happy, but it sure allows them to choose whatever misery they desire!" A rather profound truth, at that.

Maybe Holy Scripture might add a few ideas to start us thinking. "What does it profit a man if he gains the whole world and loses his soul?" or "It is easier for a camel to go through the eye of a needle* than for a rich man to enter the Kingdom of Heaven."

Oh, yes. We've heard that before, but somehow that doesn't apply to us. Or does it? What's that got to do with love anyhow?

Let's look again — "Greater love than this no man has, than that he would lay down *(give)* his life for his friend." "God so loved the world that He *gave* us His only Son."

So, What Is Love — Really?

This much we do know. God is love. God created the world out of love. Anything in this world that reflects true love

*A very low gateway in the East.

reflects God, and anywhere there is hate or selfishness He is being ignored or defied. He is love. Therefore, He can tell us about love. If we reflect a minute on His words, we find something very interesting. Those whom He condemns are people who (even though successful in this world) have not loved. Their lives have been ones of TAKING, of selfishness, God's ideal of love is obviously summed up in one word — GIVING — an unselfish, spontaneous, gratuitous giving of self without thought of repayment.

Love Is Giving

Now we have it! This is the core word — GIVING — this is love. Love is not just a daydream, a thought, a wish. Love is an *action*, an activity, a doing. But it is doing something for another, for my loved one, to make her happy, to make him happy, more secure, healthier, holier, more content. It is to do her good, good for her mind, heart, and soul. Love is *doing good for another*. It is a gift of her time, her work, her thoughts, her life, her body, to her loved one, her husband. True and perfect love is a total gift, a complete dedication, a permanent gift. It means not just that I give this and expect that in return. It means a complete free gift with no thought of repayment. Why? Because I love you! That is reason enough.

Love is gratitude. Just because you are everything you are and I have the privilege of loving you.

Not Selfish

Love is never self-centered or selfish. The moment it ceases to be a gift, freely given, and becomes something like "I want" — "I need" — "my satisfaction" — "my way" — "me" — "me" — "I" — "I"; when, in a word, it becomes plain and simple selfishness, then it ceases to be real love and, in fact, becomes exactly the opposite of love.

But Everybody Says

Strange, isn't it, how love is distorted? Our too often god-less society, our sex-saturated world has been teaching us a *lie!* It has been telling us that love is for "me," that it is sex gratification. It has taught us a code of selfishness and self-seeking that is the very opposite of real love. It has lied to us and still trumpets its lies from screen, TV, radio, and print. Sadly, tragically, too many have believed this message.

We have equated love with personal fulfillment, sex satisfaction, personal desires, and so on. We have been deceived. We have deceived each other. And we and our children are suffering the consequences.

Crumbs from the Table

This perverted concept of love is like eating crumbs that fall from the table. We taste it occasionally, but forever hunger and are not satisfied. Let us look up. In very real truth, *"Come, a banquet awaits."*

Reverie

Let's invade the privacy of a home where true love exists. Let's enter the thoughts of a husband and wife as they might pause in a moment of silence and peace and ponder what their love means to each other—Listen!
He is— She is— We are—

Sharing every aspect of our lives together.

Interested in each other's work.

Sharing our life and our love in fond closeness, a warm kiss, talking of children, of work, of problems as *our* children, *our* work, *our* problems.

Completely confident of our partner's love and our need for each other.

Truly loving each other and our children and by this finding that loving our friends and neighbors is simply a natural overflow, an easy step, to finding ourselves nearer to, and in actuality loving, God Himself.

Supremely secure and contented in knowing that I belong completely to you, and you to me; happy that it can never change, nor would either of us ever want it to change.

Giving of myself totally to you and you to me during the whole day, through our work, in our thoughts and our actions, and then at times the perfect giving in bed at night.

Busy, distracted, every minute of our lives is full, but we work together, we are buddies, we are a team.

Happy to be home at night, just so we can be together.

Wondering — what each of us did to deserve so wonderful a mate.

Grateful — because you are everything you are and you are mine.

Praying — that God will keep us alive together.

Rejoicing — in our children, our success, but knowing that no matter what reverses, failures, or tragedies occur, we still have each other and that is all that really counts.

Expressing our love in the wonderful, God-blessed way that has been His gift to us, in the unbounded intimacy and pleasure of the union of our bodies.

Peaceful and contented, physically, emotionally, and spiritually after this wonderful way of saying, "I love you." A total fulfillment that knows no regrets, remorse, guilt, or uncertainty, but rather a true peace of soul.

Wake Up!

Back to real life. Isn't this real life? Is it your life? Well, it could be — it is ours and that of many of our friends. This is what marriage could be, should be, ought to be. Anything less is not truly your Creator's plan for you. Anything less is crumbs from the table. You have less than this? Too sadly true for too many people. Too late? Perhaps not entirely for you, and certainly not too late for your children!

Key

And what is the key to finding this happiness? Allow us to suggest that it is understanding what love is and then truly *loving*. It takes a lifetime of practice, with halting progress at times. It means looking back over a year and saying, "Our love is growing" despite temporary setbacks.

Love, you see, *is not different* for parent or neighbor or God or husband or fiancé. Love is the same for each of these. Love is wanting the best for your loved one. Love is *giving*.

We may not be theologians, but to us, as married people, it seems clear that our ability, desire, and motivation to love others, and through them to love God, is a direct result of our capacity and ability to love each other as husband and wife. Having truly loved and been loved as persons, we seem to mature into and develop the capacity to love others.

The small child, the teen-ager, and too often the unloved and unloving adult question, "What am I getting out of life? What's in it for me?" The mature adult, secure in knowing love, should be able to look at life and ask, "What am I *giving?* What can I contribute? How can I help others?"

Teach Your Children?

Oh, yes! That is why we wrote this book. And here we are off and talking about love. Off the track? Not for a minute!

This is the heart and soul and core of all sex education. You teach by being yourself, by example, by doing—not really much at all by words.

If you parents love each other, then you will be able to truly love your children. You will educate your children to love truly by showing them in your home what true love is, by living a life of true consideration and love for each other. Anything less than this simply won't rub off. Albert Schweitzer said, "Example isn't only the best way to teach children; it's the only way." How true, in our homes, how true!

In Front of Them?

Show your children that you love each other. How will they know if they never see you show any affection? We think it very important that parents should kiss and hug in front of the children and let their delight show through. Show them that kissing and hugging belong in marriage between mothers and dads, and that it is good. Nothing makes a teen-ager's heart swell so with pride and joy as to see that their parents are still in love.

Don't misinterpret us now: we do not mean touches, exposure, or passionate involvement in front of them. We do mean simple, solid kissing and embracing and showing that this is a joy to you. (Usually you can't go too far, anyway, as one or another of the little ones tries to get in between you to get his share of loving, too!)

Show Them

In what other ways should we show our mutual love? In dozens of different ways all day long.

Does She?

Get up earlier than she would have to just to be sure he has his coffee and a good breakfast to start the day.

Tell the children that their dad is the greatest guy in the world, act like it herself, and bring them to the door with eagerness and a kiss when he gets home.

Make that special dish (even if she doesn't care much for it herself) because he likes it.

Keep his collars starched because he likes them that way, though she thinks it is unnecessary.

Try to get that little nap if needed in the afternoon so that she is a better wife and mother tonight.

Go to the game with him, or stay home with him, or talk or not talk to him, but just be with him because he wants her near.

Give him some occasional spontaneous physical show of affection — a kiss, a caress, a pat, a little tenderness when unexpected — and in front of the kids.

Put sugar in the peas for him.

Show a genuine concern for his absence, his fatigue.

Give him frequent encouragement for his doubts, weaknesses, failures (and, please — don't nag).

Primp, fix up, and try to look a little brighter and more feminine when he is due home.

Does He?

Show her that continuing tenderness that she so much wants and needs.

Tell her he loves her.

Tell her he appreciates her.

Call her when he will be home late for supper.

Bring her things — even a bag of peanuts — to show her he was thinking of her.

Talk to her about his work, let her share his goals, hopes, worries, successes, and failures.

Listen to her (even if he isn't too interested all the time and needs her occasional reminder, "Listen, Honey, this is important").

Help her at least with the "masculine" jobs about the house.

Help her, if she works outside the home, with his share of the work, not just the "masculine" jobs — and without being asked.

Compliment her hair, dress, cooking, clean home, good judgment, or whatever is appropriate — but just don't take her for granted.

Take her out sometimes just because she needs the change, even though he'd rather just sit at home.

Above all — does he so act and so treat her that his love actions in bed at night are the complete expression of the love he has shown her all day long? Too many men fail to understand why it is that their wife, whom they have all but ignored all day and evening, finds herself unwilling or unable to turn into a passion flower when they climb into bed at night. Man can, in honesty, compartmentalize his life and love actions, but woman's way is different. She must be loved a little bit all day in order to find it easy to love a lot at night.

Do They?

Support each other in front of the children.

Make simple, fair rules of conduct and order, make the children stick by them, and also stick by them themselves.

Respect authority outside the home, such as teachers, police, clergy, elected officials, etc.

Pray together with the children.

Avoid fighting and arguing in front of the children, and try to discuss and settle differences between themselves after the kids are in bed.

In a word, act toward each other every day and all day as though they are pleased and happy to be the other half of this marriage and work constantly at making it a better one.

Not All Sex?

All of the examples above are loving, but only a few of them involve sexual expression. All of them, however, show care and concern for the welfare and happiness of the loved one.

Let's show our teen-agers more about this true concept of love, of what it really is — that it is never selfish — that it is always giving — and that it encompasses a lifetime of joyful service as husbands and wives.

In a Parked Car?

One more example. Let's look again into that parked automobile. A young man has a girl in his arms. He tells her that he loves her. This love is apparently the greatest the world has ever known. It is so great that he wants her to give him her body so that he may adequately express his love to her. They are not married.

Does he really love her?

What is he asking her to do? To give away cheaply that very special gift that she has to offer her husband some day —

her virtue, her virginity. Possibly to warp her relations with her future husband some day because of guilt feelings, improper attitudes and habits regarding sex resulting from this hidden affair. Exposing her to a possible illegitimate pregnancy. Possibly asking her to violate her deep-seated moral convictions, to deny her God.

Does he really love her? Is he perhaps sincere and merely confused as to what love really is?

Or does he want his own gratification and is using her to gain it? Isn't he simply being selfish, self-centered, self-seeking? Isn't he really harming her, harming her mind and body and soul? Isn't he really using her? Doesn't he really love only himself?

The same, of course, applies if the shoe is on the other foot and she is the temptress, enticing him to eat of the forbidden fruit. The woman can be just as guilty as the man.

Protect Your Children

How can we teach our children to recognize the difference between love and self-centered sexual gratification? By *showing* them, not just telling them, what love is. By living this life of service, of generosity, of unselfishness, of giving, of devotion, of happiness.

If we show them true love, they will know — they will not be deceived by today's false prophets. They will look for, save themselves for, and eventually settle for, nothing less good and genuine than what you have taught them in your home.

Remember, love is giving — Try it!

6

Teen-age Marriages

When we wrote the first edition of this book almost twenty years ago, abortion was still illegal in all fifty states except to save the mother's life. Consequently, when an unmarried teen-ager became pregnant her choice was to marry or to have the baby out of wedlock. While abortions did occur, they were seldom available or sought.

Many of those teen-age mothers placed their babies up for adoption. Some did not marry and kept their babies. A very large number, however, did marry just because they were pregnant.

Times have changed. Abortion is legal, easily available, has increased at least tenfold, destroying the life of every third baby conceived in the US. To a significant extent, illegitimacy has lost much of its stigma. Adoptions have decreased markedly, not just because of abortion but also because more than ninety per cent of unwed mothers now keep their babies.

Teen-age marriages, because of these developments, are much less common than two decades ago. They still occur frequently, however, and therefore remain an option to be discussed. What are the pros and cons of marriage in the teen years? What are the chances for an enduring, faithful marriage?

Early Marriage vs. Education

This is not exactly a good time in history to be teen-agers. This is a time when education is needed as it has never been needed before. Do you know who our nation's unemployed are? There are some sixty-year-old men and women, and there are some forty- and thirty-year-old men and women, but a large bulk of our unemployed are under age twenty-five. In some cities a full twenty per cent of all men getting unemployment checks are healthy, strong, young men of twenty years or younger! These are the boys who dropped out of high school, often to get married, got a job at the local service station, had their baby, got laid off, and now are drawing unemployment compensation. They didn't get a high-school diploma, have no job training, are now unemployed, and are going to be a burden on society sporadically, through the rest of their lives.

They will be setting up new underprivileged homes that will often breed new poverty, ignorance, immorality, and delinquency. These are the boys and girls who should have gone on. They should have at least finished high school or trade school. They should have learned a skill, got on-the-job training, or done something to prepare themselves for the increasingly complex world which they live in.

Our advancing technological age is resulting in a permanent shortage of brains and training at the top, and a permanent surplus of unskilled labor at the bottom. This previous time-honored idea that a good man, however unskilled, could support his family if he were merely willing to work hard is less and less valid today. Our society simply needs less and less unskilled labor and we might as well recognize it. We should beat into our boys' and girls' heads the obvious fact that they must have some education or skill in the years ahead or they will simply not be able to earn a living. Everything is being automated today!

And yet in the face of this, a large number of boys and girls are not getting enough training or higher education because they are getting married too young.

Teen-age Marriages — What Chance for Happiness?

What's the prospect of happiness in a teen-age marriage today? Take a long guess! Some studies tell us that as many as seventy-five per cent of teen-age marriages eventually dissolve. Your child may have only one chance in four of even keeping his (her) teen-age marriage intact, and if it is a "shotgun wedding" the chances shrink to one in five. A major study of teen-age marriages showed that fifty per cent of these boys and girls, five years after marriage, were engaged in adulterous relations with other men and women. If so few of these marriages survive, how many do you think are happy? One of our greatest American anthropologists tells us that probably ten per cent of all teen-age marriages are happy. Ten per cent are happy! These, we are told, are the unusual, exceptional people — ones who, if they had gone on for further education, would be the leaders of our communities. But now they will never lead anyone. They will continue to slug their way through an uneducated, poverty-stricken life. They will just get by only because they are exceptional people. Now, do you want your child to marry in his or her teens?

Your Advice

Remember, you may be called on some day for advice as to whether or not a young couple should marry, perhaps because a pregnancy has occurred. Think long and hard before approving a teen-age marriage. The odds, as you see, are almost insurmountable. And think of the good of the children to come. The *only* criterion to use in advising them to marry is a firm conviction on your part that they can make a good, loving, successful marriage. The questions of "honor," and "doing the right thing by her," of "giving the child a name," and of "preventing scandal" are not sufficient reasons and should hardly be considered at all. This is a long life, and the misguided decision to make a poor marriage can ruin, not just the lives of the young couple, but those of their children and even their children's children.

If there is reasonable doubt as to the chance of a good, solid, happy, enduring marriage, there should be no marriage now. If she is pregnant, advise her to go away and have the child and let the baby be placed in a loving adoptive home. She may then come back and do a better job of creating a good home at some later date.

Even if a potential teen-age marriage (without the problem of illegitimate pregnancy) seems to be a good bet, remember this—it will be a better bet in one, two, or three years if they can wait. If they really are sincere in their love, they should want only the best for their partner, their marriage, and their children. If they can be shown that more education, more time to mature as a man, as a woman, and more responsibility and self-discipline in their lives together will result in a better marriage, then they are probably the exceptional people we have just spoken of. Bless them and bless you for helping them.

Earlier Dating — More Illegitimacy

Dating is begun earlier today than ever before in the history of our country. What used to be an accepted amount and type of boy-girl social get-together, dating, dancing, and partying at a college-age level is now practiced in high school. The norm for dating and social get-togethers between boys and girls at a senior high-school age level is now being pushed down into junior high school and earlier.

Steady dating, once considered only a preparation for marriage, is now the apparent norm in high school where almost one-half of all sixteen-year-old girls are going steady.

High-school dropouts of girls involve pregnancy in a great many cases.

Over half of the illegitimate babies born in our country are delivered by teen-age mothers.

One bride in six is already pregnant as she walks to the altar.

Anyone care to guess what per cent of men or women are virgins when they marry? We know that there is more talk than action, but clearly there's more action now than ever before.

Pretty miserable, isn't it? Worse than you thought! And remember, these are your neighbors and mine, your niece, his son, our children.

Why Is All This Happening?

What chance do many of these teen-age marriages have for happiness, for finding the true love and peace that is their God-given birthright, for producing good children, for living a long and happy life together? Let us think seriously and deeply about these problems, and ask ourselves the big question. Why is all this happening? Why is it that we now have this rapidly increasing amount of teen-age sexual activity, of illegitimate pregnancies, of abortion, of unhappiness?

Let us look more deeply.

7

Building Blocks

Why Teen-agers Have Sex

Let's step back, away from our own families and personal involvement, and take a broad look at the current social practices of our society. What are we — you and I — doing to and with our children that may be permitting, or actually fostering, the rather frightening trends toward earlier and earlier teen-age sexual activity?

We have already discussed:

Many of the attitudes and practices in our country today in regard to sexual morality, or the lack of it, that influence ourselves and our children.

The vital necessity for adequate, early, and reverent sex education of our children.

The need of parents to practice what they preach, and to live the life of love that marriage should be.

Effect of Social Customs

We would not minimize the extreme importance of what has been discussed so far. However, let's now turn to something that involves every parent and teacher in the country, that crosses all lines of race, color, creed, and social and economic levels. Let's take a close look at the current social customs and practices of our children and see whether any of them contribute to early teen-age sexual activity.

There are apparently many ways in which we aggravate problems of teen-age promiscuity. We often do this by customs that are individually innocent, seemingly harmless, or, at times, if considered separately, even good. But many of our current child-raising practices are part of a logical, progressive pattern of formation and education of our children, which prepare them for, and in some cases almost force them into, the premature sexual involvement that we so deplore.

Let us call these practices "building blocks." Each of these customs forms part of the completed building of the character that emerges as a child becomes an adult. Let us consider a few of these customs. As we construct this building you will see that we seem to be doing everything earlier and earlier than we used to.

We might say that each child climbs a ladder, beginning first with dancing and dating, that leads rung by rung up to eventual marriage. For most children this seems to take just so long, and the earlier they begin, the earlier they will top out. If the climb up this social ladder is begun in mid or late high school, the top is reached and they marry in their early twenties. If the climb up this ladder of boy-girl social encounter is begun in the sixth to eighth grade, then many will reach the top and become sexually involved in their teens.

Toys Teach

Let's start with one of these early building blocks — toys. Remember the kind of dolls girls used to have? They were little baby dolls, weren't they? And little girls loved their dollies. This was a maternal love, wasn't it? The dolls cried, said "Ma-ma," and the girls were their little mothers, gave them their bottles, and cared for them. This childhood play-world of being a mommy or a daddy was a healthy thing, emotionally speaking, because this early childish play taught that the adult goal of life was having a family and caring for babies and children. To plant in children's minds at an early age this attitude of love and acceptance of the wife-mother or husband-father roles was good.

Now what kind of dolls do little girls play with today? Adult-bodied glamour dolls. You know what these dolls are. They are dolls with high heels and nylons, sexy bodies, and huge breasts — sexually attractive playgirls. There is a boyfriend doll, a car (convertible, of course!), and scads of clothes to drape on this adult female figure. Your little girl doesn't get any actual sex stimulus from this, but you are very effectively beginning to teach this child of yours the fact that the goal of her life is to be a playgirl, with a boyfriend — not a "daddy." She starts to learn the value and purpose of lots of attractive clothes and that it is important to have a body that is (sexually) attractive to men.

The concepts of motherhood, fatherhood, family, marriage, and love do not enter the play world of the little girl with these kinds of dolls. We wonder if this type of incorrect early training does not contribute to a partial rejection in her adult life of her role as a wife and mother. It is probably one more small reason that our woman of today (or tomorrow) is restless, uneasy, and often unhappy with being "just a housewife and mother." This emphasis on clothes, body, hair, and good times is one block in the building of a selfish person in contrast to the warm, loving, giving attitudes developed in a mother-baby play relationship. We would consider this kind of modern doll-play and other types of adult glamour toys as negative building blocks in forming the adult personality.

A few days after we had mentioned this at a talk, a couple came in the office and the wife volunteered, "After your talk,

I went home, took my daughter's doll, and undressed it — I was scandalized! I took that doll and put it away in my drawer." Her husband grinned slyly and said, "No, it isn't, it's in *my* drawer!"

Dress like Mom

Now, what else is done? Girls are given clothes that are scarcely the functional clothes of years past, but rather clothes that are like mother's. This is perfectly innocent when they are small, but it is less innocent when the adult-cut outfit like mom's teasingly accentuates the budding breasts of the seventh grader. Even for the immature girl it already teaches an emphasis on personal physical attractiveness that is normally foreign to this age.

Hair

Next they may get a permanent wave. There's nothing wrong with a permanent wave, but thirty years ago there were few permanent waves in the first grade, and now there are often very few who do not have them. Yes, it may be easier to comb, it's cute, and some of you may disagree on this. However, you are introducing into your child's life a consciousness of hair and personal beauty that grows and develops. By the seventh grade if you go into a girls' restroom in school, you will hardly be able to find room in front of the mirror. Many girls by then have developed a real obsession, a premature consciousness of hair for the prime purpose of being attractive (to boys). This is often firmly rooted well before high school, often with mother's eager help. It is a bit of a paradox that by the middle and late teens the style often reverts to long straight hair.

Nylons and Little Heels

What's the next building block? Usually it's nylon panty-hose and heels. How soon? Ask yourselves—fifth grade? sixth grade? Recently we checked a bus from a sixth grade suburban school which had been chartered to go to a symphony concert, and out of thirty girls only two were not wearing adult hose and little heels.

Why do we give our young daughters hose and heels? Well, why do adult women wear them? Are they practical, comfortable, cheap? Of course not. Adult women wear them because men like to look at women's legs that are shapely and attractive. In a word, they are sexy! They are worn to please and attract men. So, should sixth graders wear them?

Training Bra!

Do you know what a "training bra" is? It's a small padded affair (about a AAA cup) to hang on a flat little chest to teach a little girl what it will be like when she finally grows big enough to have something to put in it. It is introducing her to what a "figure" does for a girl. Apparently some mothers (and manufacturers) are not content to wait until nature provides the equipment with which to teach their daughters sexual attractiveness—they have to jump the gun!

Charm School

Where do we go from here? Perhaps to "charm school." In what grade might you take a group of girls to charm school at the local department store? Sixth? Yes, commonly, or seventh. All done with the best of intentions by good mothers, so that their daughters may begin to learn some adult poise and social grace. They will learn more about dressing, how to take bubble baths ("Your skin really needs it, my dear"), etc. They will also learn to look at modeling as a possible goal in life. Several more little girls will, as a result, begin to use cosmetics, and most will be more conscious of dress, hair, face, and figure than they were before. This is introducing into an age group that should not even be thinking about it yet a consciousness of attractiveness to the opposite sex — too soon. In our book, charm school is a fine thing — for freshmen or sophomores in high school.

School or Church Dances

How about dancing for children? Here we meet real differences of opinion. Those in favor stress the development of poise, of the ability to converse with, be polite to, and generally act like ladies (or gentlemen) with members of the opposite sex. That development of the social graces is desirable, we would agree. Our comment here would simply be this: Is the sixth or seventh grade the place and time for this? Or is this too soon? Wouldn't the ninth or tenth grade be better? Dancing too early introduces into immature lives a boy-girl physical and emotional contact that is not natural. An eighth-grade boy at a dance, if left to his own natural inclinations, will usually avoid girls like the plague and play touch football over in one corner of the hall with other normal boys his age.

For him to put his arm around a girl's waist and hold her body next to his is a difficult thing to learn to do. However, when this body-to-body nearness and touch becomes a familiar and easy thing to do, then the first kiss and first embrace may occur years sooner than if the normal awkwardness of this age group had been allowed to persist naturally and had not been so thoroughly trained out by overzealous parents.

Girls Sooner Than Boys

A girl's body usually develops two or three years earlier than a boy's, and this must always be kept in mind. The average boy, if relatively untouched by the social-sexual pressures around him, will usually not spontaneously develop an interest in girls before the tenth or eleventh grade. A girl, while developing her body sooner, still will ordinarily not feel any irresistible urge to dance and date with boys before about the ninth or tenth grade. This is true, however, only if there are no well-intentioned youth groups, school personnel, parents (usually mothers), or progressive girlfriends pushing for these activities. These early feelings of attraction to the opposite sex are legitimate and good, and contribute to the mature development of a secure adult if they are properly channeled and not allowed to become too adult in their physical expression too early.

Dating in Grade School

The total unnaturalness of dating before high school should be apparent to all except the most misguided parents and should need no comment here. And yet this is not an uncommon practice in some areas of our country, and great pains are taken by some doting parents to "seduce" (as one prominent psychologist calls it) little boys and girls to play-act at dating in grade school.

The Next Logical Step — Sex!

By the beginning of high school the push of the mothers particularly (and dads occasionally) to make their little girls and boys popular (translated this means "to grow up too soon") begins to have its results. The teen-agers enter what normally is a somewhat confused and rebellious time of their lives, but which now, partly because of their "training," becomes even more turbulent and often disastrous. We see serious boy-girl relationships beginning two to four years earlier than they normally would occur. Why? Because they were trained that way, of course. If through their childhood years they have been encouraged to be adults in manners, dress, and social conduct, many will begin to act physically (sexually, that is) like adults as soon as their bodies mature sufficiently.

The Spark!

Sometime, somewhere, each boy and girl will discover that it is *nice* to be near the opposite sex, to be attracted, to *want!* Having been trained to expect it, to look for it, to experiment, millions of our children today are discovering the awakening of sexual desire and gratification years before they would normally have sought each other's company. Having learned dress, charm, dancing, and dating before high school, it is perfectly logical to proceed with:

Kissing in the eighth grade

Necking and petting in the ninth grade

More passionate involvement in the tenth grade

Actual intercourse by the eleventh grade, or earlier.

By graduation from high school (if they wait that long) far too many have been sexually involved, some have had babies, many more have had abortions and some have gotten married. But just as many or more are ready for an active sex life (in or outside of marriage) in the fullest physical sense because they have already done everything else. They have passed through this time of intense pressure, when "everybody else is doing it," and can and will wait no longer.

And this premature growing up we suggest is THE MA-JOR cause of teen-age sexual activity.

We Started It!

But now you can't stop it. Once they experience the thrill of adult sexual contact (be it only a kiss), you have lost much of your control over them; and they will often take it from there. The time to stop teen-age sexual promiscuity, we suggest, is way back when you buy them their first toys and clothes. To attempt to begin to cope with these problems once they are teen-agers is often almost impossible. The only way to stop it is not to start it too soon.

Popular?

In many ways we pity the girl or boy who is too popular too soon. They usually date the soonest, marry the soonest, and often divorce the soonest.

Let us suggest that each of you reflect on the disadvantages of social popularity at too early an age. Look back to your own grammar-school and high-school friends. Which girls and boys were the first to dance, to date? Which had the prettiest face, figure, hair, and clothes? Who were the really smooth fellows (social graces, remember)? Who were the first to kiss, to neck? Who got the first car? Who smoked and drank beer first? Who told the "cute" jokes?

Now — what have these popular boys and girls done as adults, as parents? Any one or more may be the exception, but what has happened to most of them? Well, we would bet they aren't all still married to their first mate, for one thing. How many went on to college to become successful, financially, socially, or otherwise? *How many made happy mar-*

riages? By God's standards, how many are successful? Draw
your own conclusions.

Do you really want your children to be popular so soon?
Are you pushing them? or permitting too much too soon? As
one mother said, "I don't want my daughter to be a burned-
out woman at sixteen."

Like a Flower

A poinsettia, forced into premature bloom for Christmas,
will wither and fade too soon. So it is with our children. They
were made by God to grow slowly and develop physically,
mentally, emotionally, and spiritually into adulthood. Each is
like a flower, or a fruit on a tree, which must stay there as
it slowly develops in stages, normally. Our children must also,
so to speak, hang there, growing and developing in stages,
surely, securely, slowly; ripening their bodies, minds, emotions, wills and souls; hanging there yet a bit longer, until
they are fully mature, well-prepared adults; secure and capable, wise and confident, able to choose properly, and then
to give themselves completely in mature, total, sacred love
to their lifetime and eternal partner in marriage.

What to Do

How to Stop the Push into Premature Adulthood

Many answers — we certainly don't pretend to know them all but let us share the ones that we do know. There are many things to start doing, and to quit doing. Let's explore more ideas that can help prevent premature teen-age sexual involvements.

Give Them Constructive Activities

Fine! Let's think of some constructive things to do that will help train and form them into the stable mature adults we want them to be.

Athletics

Athletic activity is very important in the development of a boy into a normal man and of a girl into a healthy young woman. Fortunately the premature push into competitive sports has not affected girls as much as boys. By and large it is usually a junior and senior high-school activity for girls and is beneficial for those participating. The problem is mainly to get more girls involved.

For boys, however, this must come in stages. One major

87

mistake here is the unfortunate development in our times of organizing teams at too early an age. We are seeing our early-grammar-school boys organized, uniformed, trained, and directed by earnest dads to engage in competitive athletics. We even know of a baseball "farm club" for five-year-olds!

First of all, let us sincerely compliment the good intentions and long hours of effort that so many good men devote to this activity. Without exception, they feel that they are doing a good thing for their boys. However, to all these men of good will, please consider the following.

Almost all authorities agree that it is physically and psychologically harmful for little boys to be put into stressful competition. No less a medical authority than the American Academy of Pediatrics has condemned it. Ideally, little boys should pretty well be left to their own play, and not interfered with or organized by oversolicitous moms or dads. These early, pleasant, aimless years are and should be just that — aimless — as the little boy explores the world around him and slowly becomes a big boy. The time for real competitive athletics arrives in *junior-high and senior-high years.* Then it is desirable, important, and even vital in developing the normal masculine aggressiveness and independence that should be part of the adult man. But, unfortunately, in many areas, by eighth or ninth grade, almost all the boys have been reduced to spectators and only the few good athletes remain playing.

We should strive to get or to keep all boys of junior-high age specifically interested in sports. There should be a type or degree of involvement for almost all, irrespective of their individual athletic abilities. In these years the dads should really give of themselves to encourage and help each boy to compete, be it full competitive league play for the best athletes, or intramural or informal play for others. Let each experience the stress of competition, of being down and getting up to try again instead of being a quitter, of being one of the gang, of developing one's body, of learning to identify with men and older boys because of their masculine traits (not because they are the smoothest with the girls or know the "best" jokes).

Athletics should teach a will to win, but also respect for others and for rules of good conduct and sportsmanship. It should help to teach self-control of mind and body and, above all, an identification as a person of independence and worth, secure in his own self-esteem and masculinity.

Remember, if all the dads burn out hovering over the baby leagues which, as we have said, are largely useless and often harmful, then there will not be enough of them to help with the sports of the older boys who really need it.

Frankly, we cannot say enough good for sports and for cooperation and involvement of dads in the sports programs. However, keep these points in mind:

Let little boys be little boys.

Start sports in mid to late grades and then help the boys to a progressive degree of team play and competition as they grow older.

Involve *all* boys, if possible.

Dads should help, but not dominate.

Camping, Service, and Scouting Groups

More and more often we see these groups being intensively organized as early as the second grade by industrious mothers and dads. The eager parents herd their little lambs through every dairy and jail in town, create projects to make things and do things, and generally keep the bewildered little ones and themselves quite busy. The larger organizations have central offices that keep the leaders well informed with a constant stream of paper work. The organization oftens extends to clothes, uniforms, books, calendars, toys, toothbrushes, cookie and candy selling, etc. There are even magazines to subscribe to, written mostly for young adults but strongly pushed for even the tiny tots. (We have a quota!)

After a number of years of this premature organizing of these little people, the parents tire of it, the children tire of it, and the groups begin to dissolve. In our observation, it would seem that for every five or six troops so earnestly begun in the second grade, about one troop remains by the eighth grade. Just when these good, healthy activities are really needed for the boys and girls in grammar school and early high school, they are rejected by both children and parents because they have already done it all. They are both tired of it. The children are ready for the next step up the ladder to adult social practices, that of mixed parties, dancing, and dating — too soon!

A moment's thought might be given to the little boy groups. Many of them have den mothers, instead of fathers, who run these little troops for the first few years. Far be it from us to say that some good is not derived from this type of activity, but there are other things to consider. Our boys get precious little masculine influence in our society today. In the days before the industrial revolution, a boy grew up in the shadow of his father, helping him on the farm or in the shop. This was good, for it gave him a masculine figure, his dad, to identify with, to imitate, and to set up as his goal in life. Unfortunately, few men today are able to spend large amounts of time with their sons. As a result, the boys often grow up under almost exclusive feminine influence. Grammar school continues the pattern of mostly female teachers. Usually there are few masculine teachers until junior or senior high school. Because of this we feel it unwise to introduce the mothers into virtually any phase of boy organizations. Here, at least, the *men* should take exclusive charge.

When Should They Start?

The entire idea of starting organized activities at the early ages prevalent today is open to serious question. Let's rather begin these activities at about a fifth-or sixth-grade level, and then try to keep all boys and girls in them into their teens. Otherwise, what happens? Well, what actually has happened is this. By the eighth grade, only the few big-league survivors of the little leagues are able, qualified, allowed, or encouraged to play ball. The other boys, who are no longer involved in sports or scouts, are sitting in the stands holding hands with the former girl scouts, or maybe they are behind the stands doing more than that. They are interested in more grown-up activities — too soon!

We cannot and should not underestimate the indispensable part that sports and organizations should play in early teen masculine and feminine maturation. The tragedy of our day is that these activities are often started too soon, burn out, and then, when they are really needed to help the boys and girls, they are no longer interested in that "kid stuff."

In the early teens, boys should work and play with other boys and men. First they must grow and develop into *masculine* people — a boy's boy, a man's man, a relatively formed person who can stand alone, have independent ideas and a masculine outlook on life. Once they are old enough to be secure in their early manhood, then they are ready to begin their early associations with girls. Then this next important phase of growing up begins.

The same is true for girls. They must use their early teens to develop a feminine personality and outlook on life. They are helped in this formation by girl-girl and girl-woman associations, and they are hindered or halted in this normal feminine maturing process if they begin too many close social relations with boys too early.

Other Constructive Activities

Many excellent group activities exist: Boy and Girl Scouts, Campfire Girls, 4-H Clubs, a wide variety of athletic leagues such as Knothole Club, church- and school-affiliated groups, Boys' Clubs, service organizations, and many, many others. These should play important roles in the preteen and teen years in city, suburban, and rural areas. This thinking can and should be applied to any and all organized activities for youth.

Let us reiterate that early childhood and early grammar-school years should not be overorganized. These are years when the entire world lies before the child, and it is to be slowly explored by each child in his or her own way and at each one's own speed. There is positive good in the seeming aimlessness of these early years. We can do them harm by inserting our adult selves too aggressively into their young lives, organizing and dominating their activities.

When children evidence interest in arts, crafts, hobbies, or music, or can be gently stimulated to interest in study of science, cooking, sewing, a junior great-books program, or any other broadening and educational activity, certainly parents should in every way encourage and help them.

Your home, needless to say, should be a focal point of childhood and teen activities, most of them spontaneous and informal with mom and dad able to chat with the kids, not too much, not too little.

Mother-daughter and father-son relationships are to be warmly fostered, remembering always that as parents we should not enter their world on a too juvenile level.

Too often parents fail to listen to their children or pay attention to them. If the children are ignored constantly enough over a long-enough period of time, we often find the channels of communication slowly closing, and parents find themselves almost strangers to their children. This gap often widens to a forbidding distance in the teens, when they need our counsel the most. Parents should listen to their children, not be shocked by them, never make fun of their ideas and projects, respect and encourage them in their gradually forming independent personalities — always, however, within the rules of conduct and order expected by the parents.

Psychosexual Identity

Girls can learn to be women only from other girls and women. They cannot learn it from boys or men. They must be allowed the time to learn their own sexual identity, otherwise their psychosexual identity will be stunted and they will be unable, later in life, to relate maturely with the opposite sex.

Boys can learn to be men only from other boys and men. They cannot learn it from girls and women. They must be allowed the time to learn their own sexual identity, otherwise their psychosexual identity will be stunted and they will be unable, later in life, to relate maturely with the opposite sex.

In general, our broad suggestions in regard to all youth activities are:

Don't get too organized too soon.

Let little children remain little children.

Introduce older boys to older-boy activities and older girls to older-girl activities in the preteen and teen years.

Don't allow truly adult-type social activities until well into senior high school.

9

When They Date

When Should They Date?

As high school freshmen and sophomores, properly teen-
agers should be permitted only group dates and group parties. For instance, a parent might drive a group of girls to a
high-school dance and later pick up the same group. If they
come home paired off, then it is not group dating any longer
but individual dating. This is the time when your home will
be used, or when they may begin going to a youth-club activity in a church, school, or hall. Depending on age and maturity, many freshmen boys and girls and often a sophomore
boy will not yet be interested in this mixed-group activity
and, if not, please don't push them! These group activities
should be chaperoned. Curfew time should be sensible. Parents should bring the girls home in a group, and the boys
should also travel in a separate group.

Juniors and seniors should be allowed double dates. Solo
dating would ideally be permitted only after high-school graduation. Seniors might be allowed to solo date on occasions
but not as a routine practice.

Going Steady

What is going steady? Let's define it as the exclusive company-keeping with only one person, perhaps once or twice a
week for a few months or longer.

When is it permissible? In its proper place, it is courtship, it is a preparation for marriage, an evaluation of a partner with whom marriage could be a reasonable and possible goal within perhaps six to twelve months. If this is not possible at this time in their lives, two people should not go steady. If the terms "going steady" and "courtship" would be used interchangeably, things would be more clearly recognized for what they actually are.

Let us immediately say that just because "everybody does it" does not make it right. It certainly is often more difficult to be different, but correctness and morality are not altered by the practice of "everybody else."

Going steady is morally dangerous. This is said repeatedly, but we honestly think parents are not often aware of the true danger. There are always exceptions, of course, but the majority of teen-agers who go steady after a while find themselves "going a little farther" each time, and it is the rare young couple going steady who do not, sooner or later, indulge in sexual intimacies progressing from kisses, to touches, to.... We shall be blunt. Parents who allow their teen-agers to go steady should realize that the boy and girl face serious sexual temptation, and that the odds are high that they will sooner or later become physically intimate. We believe that such parents *share the responsibility* for whatever happens.

Going steady limits one's choice of friends. It prevents playing the field, the broad acquaintance, the fun of the gang; in a word, it prevents the full maturing of the young man or woman. Both boy and girl in this situation literally stall out in their hoped-for climb to an independent, mature adult male or female status. The boy becomes or remains immature and effeminate, a position that logically dooms him later in marriage to being just the oldest "boy" in the family, under the unnaturally dominant masculine wife who did not develop her femininity properly either.

During the teen-age years, the young person should be growing, learning, forming himself (herself), preparing for adulthood. He or she should be meeting many people, observing, learning the give and take of adult relationships, learning to judge before acting, making many decisions about his or her life ahead.

Each young woman should strive to become someone worthwhile. What will she have to offer her man, to bring into her marriage? Will she have education, talents, skills? Will she be accomplished in music, art, homemaking? Will she be a person he will want to talk to, to share ideas with? Or will she have nothing to bring into her marriage but a body, wise perhaps only in the ways of sex. If so, all we can say is "poor girl." Doesn't she know that the one thing that is common to us all is our body and its capacity to find sexual satisfaction with its opposite? Her body is replaceable at any time by another woman's body. Only *she*, herself, the person — her unique, individual, different, and precious mind and heart — is irreplaceable. This is really what he wants to share through a lifetime. We use our bodies in God's plan to express our love for each other, but they are not absolutely essential to this love. What we truly love is another *person*, not his or her body.

So let us teach our children not to stunt the growth of their minds and emotions by premature emphasis on their bodies and by prematurely going steady. Let us urge them, both boy and girl, first fully to develop the one, unique, individual person that each of them is or ought to be; and only after they have become this full person of value should they seek the steady company-keeping that will enable each to choose wisely his or her life's partner.

Movies

Now here is a real problem. How many shows are there today without a couple in bed together (not married, of course)? How often are bare breasts or buttocks shown? How often is language that "would make a sailor blush" heard? Are premarital sex, adultery, and homosexuality taken for granted? What of the violence?

Unfortunately all of the above are common fare today and your junior- and senior-high-school children will be seeing it again and again unless you really supervise this area.

TV

And what of TV? First, do you subscribe to Cable Porn and not let your children see it? What about those nights when you are not home? The damage done to children in this case can be profound.

But even some of the regular network programs are enough to do harm to those budding young flowers whom you are raising. First, the total TV exposure should be sharply limited, even if their grades are good, and even more so if not. Then monitor what they watch. A big job? You bet it is but well worth it. Finally, schedule good programs for family viewing that include sports, of course, but also other educational programs and special documentaries on the networks, public TV, or cable.

Drinking

Although some states have lowered the age for obtaining alcoholic beverages to eighteen, we think parents should hold the line through high school. It is difficult enough for high-school students to keep chaste without weakening their conscience and moral and physical control with drinks. High-school-age children need group approval more than most adults, and have a stronger urge to be part of the gang. They more easily show off to prove themselves one of the gang. But a few beers can dissolve sensible and moral judgment, and tragedies sometimes occur. We simply think that no alcohol in any form should be given to any high-school students — period.

In some families, wine at meals is the custom. Except for this, however, will many high-school students drink alcohol anyway? Yes, we understand that. But they must know that you don't approve. The very worst practice is for parents to let under-age children bring their friends home and to allow them to drink with parental approval.

Driving

In many areas of our affluent society it is very common today for a high-school boy to have a car. Let us be very definite. Ownership of a car is a privilege, not a right. Driving privileges should be quickly withdrawn for breach of your rules, such as for speeding, reckless driving, drinking, overloading, staying out too late, etc.

It is well to remember that national figures show that the typical high-school boy who gets a car drops a full grade on his report. The "B" student now becomes a "C" student. A national insurance company in a survey of its policy holders noted that almost fifty per cent of all high-school students owning cars were in the lowest quarter of their class scholastically.

We recently saw this well demonstrated. A junior boy, a "B" student, after a long, hard, campaign finally wore his father down and received permission to buy a car. His next report showed that he had dropped to a "C" average. His father simply took away the car keys. The agonized and incredulous lad was not allowed to drive until the next report had brought in his previous "B" grades again. Too tough? It makes the point. What do you think?

We all know how many boys and girls die in auto accidents each year. Perhaps we parents should think more seriously, twice and then a third time, before allowing them to get cars.

No one can conclusively prove this, but serious and well-informed authorities estimate that as high as ninety per cent of all fatal teen-age auto accidents occur with the driver having had something to drink or having smoked marijuana or taken other drugs.

A highly respected and nationally known juvenile court judge of our acquaintance has been very specific: "Teen-age car ownership is one of the chief causes of juvenile delinquency in our country today." We could do little but agree with his very firm conviction.

Much serious thought should be given by parents about whether a teen-ager should be permitted to own or have unlimited access to a car under any circumstances whatsoever. The use of the family car teaches respect for the wishes of others, responsibility, cooperation, and keeps the youngster in a controllable situation. It also allows him to save his money instead of sinking every dime into his car. How many boys are there who could not afford to go to college because they had a car to support!

Not long ago, after a talk to a high-school PTA group, a big, tough, rough-looking man came up and with wet eyes he said, "I'm a cop. Doc, you didn't say anything about cars." We hadn't. "Please, Doc, tell them about cars, not just from the other schools, our kids, too! If these parents knew what their kids did in cars, they'd be horrified. Please, Doc, tell them about cars." Enough said.

Dress of Teen-agers

Here again, let's not just drift with the crowd. One can be sharp, fashionable, cute, and attractive without being sexually provocative. Remember that short skirts, tight, breast-outlining sweaters, tight jeans, and "no bras," not to mention certain bathing suits, quite surely stir up sexual desires. If you allow your daughter to "display her wares" openly and flauntingly, don't be surprised if some boy accepts the offer. Anything so well advertised certainly must be rather cheap and easily available, he will assume, and your daughter will be the loser.

Here a father is invaluable. Often a mother can talk, direct, even shout at her daughter to dress more modestly and find her very unwilling to cooperate. As one mother said, "You can only listen to her cry so long!" However, if dad (a man no less) simply says, "Now look here, Josie! That outfit is indecent. Go change it!" the matter should be settled. (This sort of problem can be prevented before it starts if this type of clothing is not bought in the first place.)

Mother should beware of the urge to recall her own youth and beauty and to attempt now to shine vicariously in the reflected glory of her daughter. Sometimes the premature emphasis on the children having sexy clothes, hair, etc., is really the mother trying to regain her own lost sex appeal in this vicarious way. Please, mothers, resist this impluse. Think of your daughter's good first. Understand yourself.

Late Hours

Here again some cooperation is needed — some kind of parent, school, church, or community group to set some reasonable and uniform curfew for different ages. It is difficult to be a loner on this, even more than on many other things. However, the trend in our society toward allowing later and later hours for dances, parties, and dates must be seriously reconsidered.

Does a dance for teen-agers run nine to one or worse yet ten to two? Shouldn't it be eight to eleven or eight to twelve? Let's get old-fashioned and require the teen-agers to return *home* (of all places!) after the dance instead of allowing them one, two, or even three hours in which to drink, race, smoke, and make out together. Our homes should be open to them. They and their friends should be welcome enough to feel "at home" at home. Not always easy? No, but we must try. If we love them, we shouldn't allow them the temptation of those late, late hours together this early in their lives.

Should we not reconsider the spreading custom of school dances which only begin after the game? And last until? Perhaps a different night for dances is more sensible.

Consider when he brings her home. Does she open the door to an empty living room, a quiet house, with parents sound alseep, to look at that inviting sofa — and ask him in? Do you think it wise? Do you really think you love your children if you allow them this temptation? Again, we suggest that you would share responsibility for what happens.

Perhaps the old idea of waiting up for daughter (and son) needs to be resurrected. This much is sure: if you do start waiting up for them, you will set more reasonable hours and insist on their conforming!

Prom Night

We know of a city with several public high schools in which all schedule their junior-senior prom on Friday night with little thought of any after-hour control of the students. It is near an area of lakes and cottages, and the custom has grown to move from dance to cottages for all-night or all-weekend parties. And this, we understand, with the active help and cooperation of many of the parents! We might hope this is a tragic exception to the rule, but, sadly, we know differently.

Let's remember what the mentality of prom night is. It's like the night before he shipped out, the last time they saw each other. What was the feeling then? Tonight is different! Anything goes! All restraints to the wind; I love you! Pardon the comparison, but high schoolers sometimes act this way on prom night.

The Christian high school in the above city, in an attempt to protect its students, schedules its prom on a weekday night with a suggested curfew and enforces class attendance the following day, expelling any student who is absent without legitimate medical reason. This same school attempts to instruct the parents and students as to the reasons for these rules. We can only warmly commend a wise principal who is trying. His chief problem is not that many students rebel — that he expects — but that many parents not only do not cooperate, but deliberately lie in writing in the notes they send with their children to school in reporting the reasons for their absence the following day!

This night, of all nights, they need to be protected from themselves. They need specific hours and chaperones. Lots of good fun, later than usual, of course, but precious little chance to spend much time alone together.

Skating Parties, Football Games, Etc.

Wonderful! A group activity. Come and go in groups if ninth and tenth graders, as double dates if eleventh and twelfth graders. Boys and girls mix while there, or in a home or ice-cream parlor afterward. This is good, healthy growing up.

Slumber Parties

Appropriate in high school years. Only girls, of course, and a fair but definite time for "lights out." The mothers must remain physically present and no — we mean no — boys should be allowed in.

This Means You

We could go on, and so could you, examining the various boy-girl social activities of our time. We have discussed this largely from a middle-class view because this applies most directly to most of our readers. The general principles we feel are just as valid, however, for both prince and pauper, and we ask you to consider these principles in the context of your area, race, religion, education, work, or economic condition.

Remember, when we tamper with nature's normal step-after-step development, and insert, allow, or force one or many activities into our children's lives too *prematurely*, they usually *pay the price* sooner or later in social, psychological, or marital grief.

10

Self-control

Self-control Today

Self-control is an unpopular phrase in these times. The emphasis today is on self-expression. Do not get frustrated. It is all relative. Anything is really all right as long as you don't hurt another person, and even that often is questioned. "I am entitled to sexual fulfillment, no matter what my position in life happens to be. I cannot do without this. It is my just due."

This attitude is a mixture of half-truths, wishful thinking, muddled morals, and twisted logic. We would firmly reject this current "liberated" thinking. Certainly at one time or another people have perhaps overemphasized self-discipline, but, without doubt, we feel that the more recent deemphasis on self-control has been a great mistake.

There is no physician or psychologist in the business of talking to and helping troubled people who is not very much aware of guilt conflicts, repressions, and frustrations. These are real problems and often major ones. They must be helped, treated, prevented. However, we do not prevent frustrations merely by an attitude of total permissiveness, for this will instead simply engender future, deeper, and more agonizing frustrations.

Nature of Man

You have heard the saying, "God always forgives. Man sometimes forgives. Nature never forgives." It is the nature of an animal not to have a free will, and, therefore, it acts naturally in acting according to its instincts. Man, however, by nature and God's design, has the ability to make free decisions above and beyond the mere urgings of his or her bodily desires and instincts.

This greater power and privilege of mind and will brings with it the responsibility and need to use these faculties properly, according to a higher plan than that of the animals. We have the ability and power of self-control and are most human when we use it properly, and more the instinctive animal when we do not.

When to Start

The time to begin training in self-control is when the child is very small. For the toddler it is best simply to baby-proof the house and let it go at that. For the preschooler make a few rules — simple, clear, definite — and stick to them. There should be a few absolutes, but not many. For instance, in our house we have an absolute interdict on any child biting another person. This calls forth an immediate spanking. It does not matter if his buddy did just clobber him with a toy truck. Biting is an absolute no-no! It is never an acceptable means of retaliation. He learns very early a little self-control. You may decide that playing with knives, matches, running into the street or other actions might be also absolute no-no's, but don't make too many of them.

Adults also have a few absolute no-no's, particularly in sexual, legal, and monetary relations to others, and some of these must be learned early.

Allow creativity and latitude in many things, as long as they do not infringe on the rights of another. When your children are small, use simple, short sentences in your explanations and directions so they can clearly understand you.

Give them a chance to choose, even if it is only the color of ice cream they want. Freedom of choice and self-discipline are parts of each other.

Consistent

Be consistent. If it is OK today, then it should be OK tomorrow, too. Husband and wife should have a united front in matters of teaching or discipline and should not contradict each other in front of the children. A home where there is consistency (for example, boh parents being strict or both being lenient) can and does commonly produce well-balanced children. However, if there is conflict and division of authority, where dad says "come" and mother says "go," where one parent sides with the child against his mate, then this home will often produce neurotic children.

Discipline Little Children

When administered, discipline should be firm, honest, direct, reasonable, and prompt. We should avoid bitterness and mental punishment. The silent treatment is unwise, harmful, and should not be used. Remember always to punish the little culprits but still to love them. Never withdraw your love for the little culprit: you dislike only the action, the offense. Try not to get angry with your child because, if you punish in the heat of your anger, your punishment is vindictive, not constructive, and he or she learns little to correct the wrongdoing.

Reassure them of your love and concern for them. Tell them that you are trying to train them to grow up to be good big-people, and that it is your God-given duty to make them behave. You punish when needed, but you do it out of love for them and you must clearly tell them this or they may not know.

Value of Things

Your child should be taught the value of material goods. Money, clothes, and cars don't just grow on trees, and children should be taught responsibility in using this world's gifts. If a child breaks a toy and wants it replaced, what should be done? Was it an accident? If so, probably replace it, but only after a wait. Let her know a little want, a little deprivation, so that she will be more careful the next time. Did she break it purposely? Then she will not get another for a long time.

Toys

In fairness to the children please do not get them the cheap, ready-to-break, come-apart-plastic, or the complicated, expensive, just-push-the-button toys that are so common today. Get them simple, nonbreakable, wood or metal, creative toys. Perhaps the most used and useful toy we ever gave our children was a set of homemade blocks. We bought five regular 2 × 4 pieces of pine lumber ten feet long. Then using the width (the 4-inch measurement) as a unit, plus a hand saw (and a lot of sawing), daddy and his "helpers" made a set of building blocks of varying sizes, of ½-, 1-, 2- and 4-unit lengths and several angle pieces. These proved to be indestructible and were used almost daily for years. The children showed untold creative imagination to build cities, houses, fleets, forts, dinosaurs, car washes, armies, etc. Frequently enough, other neighbor children abandoned the overmechanized toys that adults had thought up, and came to play with our simple blocks with which they could work, play, dream, and create.

Conscientious Deprivation

Don't get your daughter more clothes than she really needs. Do not always give in to your children's request for candy or ice cream, another dime or dollar. Teach them the value of things. Let them be a part of your charitable giving to others. Before Christmas, perhaps, make a practice of each child (and yourselves) giving some worthwhile toys, clothes, or something of value to the "poor children," the missions, Goodwill, or like agency. Teach them to give to those less fortunate a share of the gifts God has given to them.

Tell them that your daughter's pretty face or your son's brains are not of their own creation. God gave these gifts, and if He gave more to some than to others, He expects more from some in return. Tell them — show them. Remember the parable of the talents?

Money

Everyone can strive for an adequate job, income, and security. For some, however, this is never quite attained. Why? Obviously health, lack of education, bad luck, and various problems conspire to keep some families in an underprivileged state. However, for most people these times have been good, *if* they have not set too high a financial goal in life. You know the old story. "We'd be in good shape if only I'd make ten per cent more." If he did, he would soon be needing another ten per cent — and another. We admit wide differences among people as to legitimate desires, needs, and abilities. But, money should never be your criterion for happiness. It should be considered not as an end in itself but only as a means to an end. Let us live relatively simply and not be conspicuous or gaudy in displaying what we have. Homes, furniture, and clothing should reflect simple, solid, honest values and tastes. Avoid flamboyant, external show and facade, which too often masks an uncertain, insecure, or even decadent interior.

In the Book of Deuteronomy God told the Jews to give

one-tenth of all they possessed. Today, even though percent-
ages and possessions are qualified by income tax, family needs,
and other responsibilities, we all share the responsibility of
helping those less fortunate than ourselves. So remember to
give back to God (or His creatures) a portion of what He has
allowed you to earn. Teach your children the true place of
money and material goods in God's plan. Teach them to use,
control, and share what they have and are given, not to abuse
it.

Discipline Teen-agers?

Many parents in our modern society are unsure of just
how far to go in enforcing discipline or enforcing rules of
conduct for their teen-agers. The children, of course, rebel
and vocally protest any infringement on their freedom. Ideas
of allowing self-expression and development, of not repress-
ing or frustrating personality developments, are at least
vaguely present in the minds of all parents. The very real
question, therefore, is whether it is helpful or injurious to the
child in his teens to enforce definite parental discipline and
authority.

The concept of allowing self-expression has definite value
and importance, but should not be given complete free rein.
One could note the opinions of such men as Erik Erikson,
who speaks as one of the contemporary authorities on youth
in social-psychological matters. He tells us that the existence
and enforcement of definite parental rules of social and moral
behavior are necessary and important in the maintenance
and development of a basic sense of security and identity
during the slow emergence of the independent adult personality. Teen-agers will usually question, challenge, and often
resist parents' authority, but deep down inside they need the
security of a firm hand of guidance and are really very lost,

unhappy, and insecure if they are allowed complete freedom. Remember, however, they'll never admit it.

As always, the wise leader (parent) is not a dictator. He or she will make a few definite rules on important matters which must be obeyed, and then allow considerable latitude for each child to make many lesser decisions for himself or herself.

Finally, Self-discipline

Some day, each child is apt to find himself (herself) in a compromising situation. Each will have to make a free decision that will influence his (her) life and that of another person. Each will, one or many times, be in a position of sexual temptation, alone or with a partner. The decision as to what is right or wrong is a decision of each one's mind, morals, and religious belief. If, however, one knows this action is wrong but *wants* to do it anyway, then enters the question of self-control, self-discipline.

Has a child by this time gained the self-mastery that is so important? It will not suddenly hit him or her out of the blue. No, self-control in this situation is the result of hundreds and thousands of small and large individual acts of self-control that he or she has performed in the process of growing up. Children are trained to master themselves by the entire process of rules, love, attitudes, discipline, order, and authority in the home. If thus far through life, he or she has never been asked to deny wishes for candy, dress, toys, sleep, food, or any other self-indulgence, then how and why would this young person resist a sexual pleasure now so much wanted? His illicit pleasure and perhaps her illegitimate pregnancy is, in fact, attributable to parental indulgence and a failure to teach discipline of self.

After They're Married

Then there is no more need for self-control? We know better, of course. But often enough the teen-agers of today think otherwise. There is a considerable body of thought to-day that would grant unlimited freedom of sexual expression in marriage anytime and always. This is just not so. True, in marriage we enjoy the full privileges of each other's bodies in expressing our love for each other. But for many different reasons, there are times when one desires this union but cannot have it. At these times one must use self-control and wait. So this art of self-mastery is a continuing fact during our entire lives — not just sexually but in many other ways.

The point here is that many young people underestimate the necessity of self-discipline because "as soon as we're married, we'll be permitted to do everything." Better straighten them out! Marriage does solve some problems, but new ones arise, and each person remains the same person who origi-nally said, "I do."

The time for children to grow in self-control starts way back and parents have the watering can.

It isn't easy — but never quit trying!

11

Answers

A Loving Home

True love lived vibrantly in a happy, secure home is basic. A home with an atmosphere of peace, unselfishness, generosity, and devotion between husband and wife produces children who are capable of recreating in their own marriages the kind of home from which they have come. Almost no amount of training and teaching can straighten out a personality warped by an upset, unloving, strife-torn home life. Similarly, in spite of pressures and human problems, very few crises in life can destroy or shake the inner security, the ability to love and be loved, that is formed in the roots of one's being by a good home.

Look at Yourselves

The first job, then, fellow parents, is to perfect yourselves and your own marriage. Look deep into yourselves and ask what can be improved in your marriage. The first person to change is *you*, Bill (or *you*, Joan), and not your partner. Ask yourself, "What can I do to make our marriage happier? Do I love truly? Have I been sufficiently *unselfish*? Have I truly *given* of myself?" And of course, each partner must do the same soul-searching.

Communication

Husband and wife must talk together about life and love, work and play, God and children, money and relatives, sex and politics, and all the real things of life that should be shared together but that so often tear them apart. Slowly, charitably, kindly, respectfully, find your agreements and disagreements, and each then must "give" a bit, and then a bit, and yet a bit more. This is not easy. It takes time. It means self-sacrifice, which may be at times downright painful. But peace and happiness are found in unselfish love. Love is giving and this giving can be joyful if done right for, really, in *giving* we receive.

Remember, nothing very constructive is ever gained by a discussion between you if one or the other is too rigid, too "right," too prejudiced. Arguing and raising your voices usually defeats any chance of finding a solution. Tears rarely help. Nor does avoiding the issue.

The crux of a solution to any misunderstanding between husband and wife is the realization by each that usually *neither can win*. Their common ground is usually a compromise. Each gives up something, not grudgingly, but generously because "I love you."

Religious Faith

Some of you may think that we have talked too much of God in this book. We have simply been honest. The concept of God is an ever-present reality in our lives and we commend it to you. We are deeply aware of our own weaknesses, deficiencies, and recurrent lapses, but also hope that some day God will give us "A" for effort. Our faith has been a constant source of strength and joy for us, and we hope it will also be for our children. We hope that it will provide for them, in their years of dating, courtship, and marriage, the strength, solace, and help that it has been for us.

Whatever your creed, we are sure that the overwhelming majority of you readers share with us our desire for premarital continence, marital fidelity, and a lifetime of happiness for our children. We are deeply convinced of this. We suggest to you that, when passions are aroused before marriage, and that powerful sexual urge says, "Let's do it," few defenses are so effective as a deeply ingrained sense of moral right and wrong, of knowledge of God's love for us, but also of His justice.

Let us teach our children more about God. Not just a towering, distant, authoritarian figure. Not just negatives, and "Thou shalt not." Not just don't, don't, don't. Let us tell them that God is our Father in heaven who loves us. Show them what love is. Give them reasons for human dignity. Show them the value of personal virtue, the value of their bodies. Act in our homes all day and all week long like God-fearing people, not just on Sunday, or when it pleases us.

Show them by your life that to obey His laws is not a chore to be done grudgingly, but a real privilege and a joy. Show them that right actions bring happiness and peace, and that wrong actions bring chaos, grief, and unhappiness. Show them!

We Must Grow!

We parents must use the many means available to better ourselves so that we may better help our children. How? Well, reading is one very important way to develop and perfect yourselves. You have read this book to the end. Good. Now go out and get the next, and the next. We have listed a few good books relating to our subject in the bibliography and there are dozens of others.

Continue to read....

Study Groups

This truly adult formation and information movement is growing rapidly and has an explosive potential for good in our society. Its pattern is variable. Basically, it usually consists of several couples, perhaps five or six, who meet regularly (e.g., every other week) in each other's homes to discuss a predetermined subject of family life, religion, social problems, politics, etc. We personally urge you to organize or join one. You and your children will both be richer for it. For what it's worth, this book would probably not exist except for the fact that we were invited to visit one such group eight years before we wrote this and thought we would go "just once." We can't overemphasize the importance of this type of adult investigation and learning about a subject; of group decision as to a need or problem; of specific action taken by the group. Observe — judge — act.

For those of you who have experienced the joys of true love and who have the ability to teach others, we urge you not to hide your light under a bushel but to share it with others. You will find that your personal gain will be greater than whatever help you might feel you have given others.

Get Organized — The Children Are

As parents, we too commonly face each problem and decision alone, while the children have long since decided what they want. We should get together as parents. Let's face our problems together, be frank, discuss them, understand them. Then, as *groups of parents*, let's make certain decisions, rules, some guidelines for the benefit of our children that will fit our times, our religions, and our community.

This parental cooperation could be as official as a community code of conduct sponsored, perhaps, by a Kiwanis group, in a religiously pluralistic area. It could be a PTA or a church group. It might be the parents of one class. It could be a local couples' study group. It could be just the five parents of the five sophomore girls who chum together who agree on the type of dating, curfew time, etc., for their daughters.

Do Something

The important thing is — *do* something! Don't just drift with the current of present-day social practices, or in the rapids ahead may be a tragedy that will wreck your child's life and chance for future happiness.

Remember, you and your children will have to be *different.* It has often been that way. The crowd is too often wrong. Our job will be easier, however, and more successful if we are not the only loner in the whole group. If we can gather a small earnest group of like-minded people around us for support; if our child has a similar group to identify with, to help each other, then the going will be easier.

Remember Noah and the flood? He was a loner, but he was right. Remember Jesus alone on the cross?

Just a few of us to support each other, to direct our precious children onto the right path, that is all we need — a few good people working together to begin these changes — plus a little help from HIM.

For Parents and Teachers

NEW

THE ANSWER TO SEX EDUCATION IN SCHOOL

FINALLY

a reasonable middle-of-the-road answer

READ

this carefully before you do anything in your school

$4.95

FOR
- All School Officials
- All Teachers
- All Parents

In simple, direct fashion, Dr. and Mrs. Willke have again distilled their years of study, lecturing, traveling, and consulting throughout the U.S. and Canada on the subject of sex education in school.

Materials on this and following pages available at your book store or order direct include postage $.75 per single book or unit

HAYES PUBLISHING CO.

6304 Hamilton Avenue —Cincinnati, Ohio 45224—
Phone (513) 681-7559

For Students and Young Adults

A live recording of a dialogue between Dr. and Mrs. Willke and 500 college students. The question? If an enduring marriage is your goal would some experience in intimate sex before marriage be wise?

Considering only medical and psycho-social aspects they establish rapport, discuss, explain and analyze, finally, with the students, concluding that for most, it is smart to wait.

Cassettes
    4 sides with manual $13.95

$2.95

SEX & LOVE
explores the
dating years

MARRIAGE
a short
pre-marriage
course

$2.95

For Preschool to Adolescent

HOW BABIES GROW

• For preschool to adolescent
• A sensitive telling of the beautiful story of conception to birth. 10 min., 18 slides
• 10 min., 21 slides, audible & electronic beeps

$17.95

THE GERMAN EUTHANASIA PROGRAM

EXCERPTS FROM "A SIGN FOR CAIN"

FREDRIC WERTHAM, M.D.

. . . . the Euthanasia Program that was conceived and carried out by German doctors from 1939 to 1945. The express purpose of this program was not to kill Jews, Gypsies, Poles, and other non-Aryans, but rather to purify the German race by the direct killing off of pure blood German citizens who were physically, emotionally, or mentally defective.

$1.25 ea.

Pro Life Materials by Dr. & Mrs. Willke

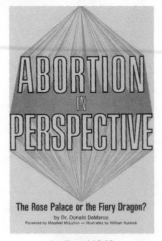

hardbound $8.00
paperback $5.95

by Dr. Donald DeMarco

A fascinating collection of ideas by a brilliant thinker. Dr. DeMarco's incisive thought essays pierce to the core of the philosophical and ethical aspects of the life issue.

— not a rerun of what has been said before, but some entirely new insights!

FOR
— every thinking pro-life person
— every college and church every library

ABORTION, HOW IT IS

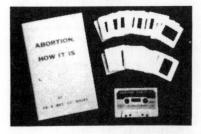

This is the startlingly effective presentation by the Willkes that has had such a profound influence on the abortion debate in the U.S. and Canada.

42 MINUTE VERSION, 35 slides, Manual

One Cassette { Side one, 26 min. on Human Life
Side two, 16 min. on Abortion

15 MINUTE VERSION, 35 slides, Manual

One Cassette, 15 minutes

Either version *$24.95*

Spanish } *$19.95*
French

Swedish, Portuguese } *$24.95*
German, Italian

32 min. Cassette, 24 Slides,

42 min. Version

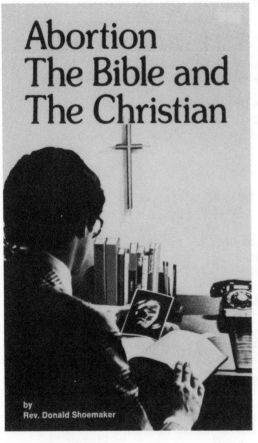

Library Pack

The best of the pro-life books to balance the everpresent pro-abortion books on the shelves. Selected by the National Right to Life Education Committee.

Handbook on Abortion
Abortion in Perspective
Abortion and Social Justice
German Euthanasia
Aborting America
A Private Choice

} all six hardbound $33.00

Handbook on Abortion (Spanish)
Right to Live, Right to Die
Population Growth
Abortion--Silent Holocaust
Abortion, Bible, and Christian
Psychological Aspects of Abortion

} may be added $27.00

New Perspectives on Human Abortion
Death, Dying and Euthanasia

} separate listing $25.00

Pro Life Materials by Dr. & Mrs. Willke

The Brochure that reversed
opinion in Michigan
to a pro-life majority
in their referendum.

Available in
English
Spanish
French
German
Italian
Portuguese
Dutch
Norwegian
Hungarian
Polish
Japanese
Chinese
Swedish
Turkish

Full color
for mass
distribution.

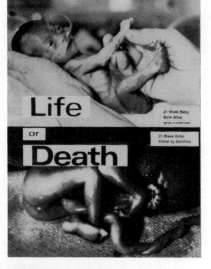

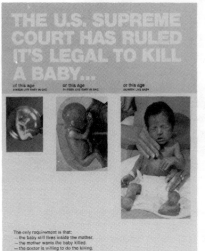

100 copies .... 14 ¢ each
1,000 copies .... 10 ¢ each
10,000 copies .... 7.5 ¢ each

Supreme Court brochure,
available in English language
only, to be used after they have
seen LIFE OR DEATH.

Full color
for mass distribution.

Pro Life Materials by Dr. & Mrs. Willke

DID YOU KNOW

This is how big you were when you were only 11 weeks old. From then on you breathed (fluid), swallowed, digested, urinated, and had bowel movements, slept, dreamed, and awakened, tasted, felt pain from touch and heat, reacted to light and noise, and were able to learn things.

After 11 weeks no new organs began functioning; you just grew more mature.

AN ENVELOPE STUFFER
—A MINI BROCHURE *in English, Spanish, French, German, Italian, Portuguese, Croation, Swedish.*

100 copies	4.5¢ each plus post.
1,000 copies	3.5¢ each plus post.
10,000 copies	3¢ each plus post.
100,000 copies	2.5¢ each plus post.

Brief, hard hitting facts on development in the womb.

Envelope size.

Easy to include with every letter, bill, or mailing you send.

Pass out at a sports event, a fair, or a convention, at an abortion clinic.

WALL POSTERS 24" x 36"

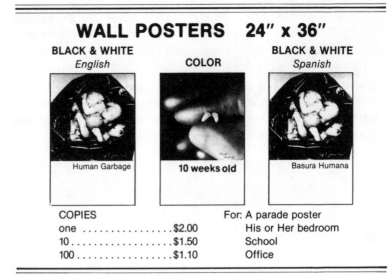

BLACK & WHITE
English

COLOR

BLACK & WHITE
Spanish

Human Garbage

10 weeks old

Basura Humana

COPIES
one	$2.00
10	$1.50
100	$1.10

For: A parade poster
His or Her bedroom
School
Office

DR. and MRS. J.C. WILLKE

Both are graduates of the University of Cincinnati, she from the College of Nursing and Health, he from the College of Medicine. Mrs. Willke taught her profession for five years, chairing her department in a College of Nursing, before her full-time career as wife and mother. Dr. Willke has been a practicing physician for 33 years, is a diplomat and Fellow of the American Board of Family Practice, devoting much of his time to teaching and family counseling. He is on the Senior Attending Staff of the Providence and Good Samaritan Hospitals. He is a certified Sex Educator and Counselor and an accredited Family Life Education Supervisor. They have six children, ages 19-33.

Internationally known experts in human sexuality, the Willke's lecture throughout the United States, Canada, and Europe. In an average year they will speak in 50 cities, face 50,000 people and appear on over 100 radio and T.V. programs. Their articles have appeared in over forty publications. They have written many books and made several tapes and recordings.

The Willkes lecture to groups of physicians, teachers, clergy and professionals in many allied fields as well as to major parent and university audiences.

Members and consultants to local, state, national, and international organizations in the field of medicine and human sexuality, their professional qualifications are greatly enhanced by their own deeply fulfilling love shared in an exceptionally good marriage.